Into the Light

More Swadlincote Stories

Monica Hudson
Joan Jones
Roland Toon
Eileen Harvey
Christine Liversuch

Published by South Derbyshire Writers' Group, The Cottages, 6 Church Street, Swadlincote, Derbyshire, DE11 8LE

© Text: Contributors

Photographs: Eileen Harvey (Ration books, Eileen & Doug Harvey). Arthur Rice (A Rice Captain, Flying Group, Hull of Friday, Plane Halifax, Newhall Homeguard; J.Hassell, B.Laxton, E.Johnstone, A Rice). Gladys Adams nee Jones. Roland Toon (Roland Toon). Doctor Goodacre (Swad. Surgery). J Jones (Local road 1947, Hill St. 1930's, Ray Evans, William Parry, Brian Holins and staff, Bretby Hospital, Simon Wardle, Peter P & R meats, Dorothy Smith, Keith and Di Oakley, Jill Jacobs, Brenda Maddock, Dorothy Gough, Children playing instruments, Pingle school band, New Delph market, World war two display). Ray Evans (Paramount Car). John Baumgartner (1987 Baumgartner Shop and staff). Mr Dinnis (sen) (Mr Dinnis, Simon and Freda). Monica Hudson (Old Shoddy). Burton Mail (Last Shift at Rawdon, Princess Anne, Swaddie, Children time off to Greet Diana, Alan Hodgins with Shirley Pickess, Princess Diana and Richard Smith, TG Green Director, Polly Jemison and Lucy Gannon, Face in the crowd). Paul Dowling (Jack Chariton). Paul Glover (Salts Staff). Joan Bennett (Louisa meets Princess Diana, Louisa places flowers). Jean Toon (Bill Toon). Vince Whitewood (On the piste). Mrs Doyle (T Greaves, P Cowlishaw, H Pickering). Mr Marclou (Newhall Brass Band 90's). Roy Davies (Gresley Boy's Choir). John Parkinson Hardman (Joanna Parkinson Hardman). Andrew Booth (Andrew Booth). Mrs Sommerbell (Jennie Summerbell). Mrs Jones (Carl Jones).

Cover Design: Richard Mansfield

ISBN: 0 9536288 0 9

Printed: Solus, Robian Way, Swadlincote, Derbyshire, DE11 9DH.

The book has been funded by Awards For All. South Derbyshire District Council, Literary Development fund and South Derbyshire Coalfields Rural Initiatives Fund.

This book is the third in a series of projects initiated by South Derbyshire Writers' Group on Swadlincote and the South Derbyshire area. The First, 'Swad Words, Swad Pictures' was a project funded by South Derbyshire's Council for Voluntary Services, South Derbyshire District Council's Arts Development Grant and the Coalfields Rural Initiative Fund 1998/9. This involved professional photographer, Chris Beech working with the group to devise a series of photographs based upon the edited 'voice' of the local people. South Derbyshire District Council's Literary Development and East Midlands Arts funded the publication of the resulting book 'Out of the Dark'.

The second project, 'Sounds Like Swad', was made possible through a successful application to the National Lottery's 'Art For Everyone Express Scheme'. This allowed for the group to learn radio writing and production skills in the development of an hour long audio programme. Writer and broadcaster, Graham Sellors worked with the group on the project which blends local speech with a scripted narrative.

Research for 'Out of the Dark', Sounds Like Swad, and now 'Into the Light 2000' have created a collection of tangible memories. Taped voices, typed words and photographs from this area that we feel should be shared with everyone. A Heritage Archive?

For further information on literature and Community Publishing in the area contact:

Literature Development, Derbyshire County Council, Libraries and Heritage Department, County Hall, Matlock, DE4 3AG. Tel: 01629 580000.

South Derbyshire Writers' Group would welcome anything of interest to local readers, contact treasurer, Monica Hudson at: The Cottages, 6 Church Street, Swadlincote, Derbyshire, DE11 8LE. Tel: 01283 225729.

People Express are the Community Arts organisation for the area and will provide help and advice on projects in many art forms including literature and photography. Contact: People Express Arts, Gresley Old Hall, Gresley Wood Road, Swadlincote, Derbyshire, DE11 9QW. Tel: 01283 552962.

CONTENTS

Contributors   5
Foreword   7
Introduction   9

chapter one
Through the War   10
Walls Have Ears   11
Sent to the Country   33
Cloak and Dagger Stuff   43

chapter two
Exciting Years   54
The Bone Setters   66
Swad's Pride   73
Going Going Gone!   100

chapter three
Life After Salts   106
All Change   107
A Right Royal Welcome   116
Get Your Skis On!   146

chapter four
History in the Making   150
Yee Hah!   159
Swadlincote's Stars   165
The Millennium Dawns   182

4 • THANKS

The South Derbyshire Writers' Group would like to thank the following:

The Awards for All team in Nottingham, Graham Hunt at South Derbyshire Coalfields Rural Initiative Fund, not just for the funding but for their help and encouragement.

South Derbyshire District Council's Leisure Services Committee, with special thanks to Councilor Mike Lauro for his encouragement throughout the project to bring Swadlincote 'Out of the Dark' and 'Into the Light 2000'. All the team in the Leisure Services Department particularly Stuart Batchelor. The lovely 'voices' on the front desk, Jo, Julie, Kay, Mandy.

District Librarian Polly Jemison, Librarians Sue Peach, Margaret Dean, Assistant Librarian Chris Chandler and all the staff at Swadlincote Library who have assisted us in many ways with all our projects and workshops.

Many local individuals and organisations have given us support as a group and with the project. Brian Vertigen at the *Burton Mail* and the staff in the Swadlincote Office. The Mercury New Shop, Steve and all the staff, for selling 'Out of the Dark', 'Sounds Like Swad' and for promoting this one while it was still an idea. We thank Graham Sellors for allowing us to use some of his material and contacts from 'Sounds Like Swad'. The very helpful and supportive staff of the Swadlincote Branch of Alliance and Leicester plc. Iris at Rink Print. Swadlincote's Trident Housing Association for assisting in expanding the group by allowing us to use one of their community rooms for workshops and meetings free of charge.

A huge thank you to Richard Mansfield, Deputy Head of Pennine Way Junior School for his time and patience with us in his production of the wonderful cover to this book.

We would like to thank all those who loaned and allowed us to copy their precious photographs, pictures of Swadlincote's past and the intriguing prospects for the future. Special thanks to Ray Evans - The Paramount Car. Paul Dowling - Green Bank Leisure Centre. Vince Whitewood - Swadlincote Ski Centre. Mr Dinnis, Simon Dinnis - Dinnis HB & Son. Mr John Baumgartner, Mr Hillstone - Baumgartner Frank & Sons. Mrs Baumgartner. Brian Hollins and Staff- Lloyd's Cycles. Mr Richardson Boss - Richardson Furnishing, for their help and kindness in providing us with details which would otherwise have been lost for ever.

A big thank you to everyone who have contacted us in any way with information and encouragement by letters, telephone calls or personal contact. We are very grateful for all your help with this project.

CONTRIBUTORS • 5

John Bailey
Graham Nutt
Eileen Harvey
A Timms
Nita White
John White
Ron Edmonds
Claire Edmonds
Vera Eames
John Wilson
Reg Reed
Pat Cowlishaw
Arthur Rice
Dorothy Gough
Paul Liversuch
David Liversuch
Christine Liversuch
Roland Toon
Pat Raynesford
Brenda Weber
Pat Hawkins
Mary Hawkins
Gladys Jones
Jenny Burley
Freda Goodall
John Budsworth
Burton Mail
Reg Large
Brian Hollins
John Baumgartner
Mr Hillstone
Mr H B Dinnis
Simon Dinnis
Polly Jemison
Mr Richardson Boss
Bill Jones
R Pointon

W E Grice
Monica Hudson
E Hurdman
N Yenning
J T Bradford
P Wright
E Sutton
F Dyke
G Betteridge
Paul Glover
Nancy
L J Bennett
Joan Bennett
R Evans
Jean Toon
Belinda
L Hardman
Mrs Galer
Vera Archer
R Hunt
R Jones
Mr Murfin
Graham Sellors
Joan Jones
Mark Todd
R Mansfield
Emily Zara
Daniel Zara
Simon Wardle
Peter P&R Meats
Dorothy Smith
Keith Oakley
Di Oakley
Jill Jacobs
Brenda Maddock
Klara McDonald
Mr Hextall

Eric Jacks
Joan White
Walter White
Shirley Pickess
Alan Hodgkins
Linda Smith
Mr Marclou
Newhall Brass Band
S Jones
Pingle School Big Band
Joanna Parkinson
Hardman
Andrew Booth
Reg Yates
Jennie Summerbell
Carl Jones
Mr and Mrs Jones
T Greaves
H Pickering
Michael Pattinson
Richard
Michelle
Sarah
Becky Storie
Katy Storie
Mellissa Howard
Mathew
Michelle
Kelly
Lois Print
Jessica Eley
Lucy Gannon
E Johnstone
Roy Davies
Gresley Boys Choir
K Brennan
Iris - Rink Print

FOREWORD • 7

The first publication of the South Derbyshire Writers Group "Out of the Dark" was received with great enthusiasm locally and considerable critical acclaim from further afield.

It was an instant 'best seller' in book form and was serialised in the local press and on Radio Derby. the oral version in local dialect was also a great success.

There is little doubt that the quality of that production was a major reason that the Writers Group secured an Arts Lottery award to help finance their latest work entitled "Into the Light 2000."

This book continues to record memories of life around Swadlincote and its environs from wartime to present day, recalled by the people who experienced it. As the title suggest it also looks to the future with items on young people.

In fact the titles of both books are intriguing. Are we really emerging from dark into the light?

Certainly our pavements no longer ring to sound of boots of miners going on shift to hew a living from the dark bowels of the earth. Pottery kilns and chimneys no longer spew forth their black pall over our towns and villages. Smog is a memory of the past!

I look around our District now and see the giant earthmovers shaping the land, forthcoming parks, lakes and recreational areas. Evidence of the National Forest, which will herald a new future for a new generation of South Derbyshire People, is all around.

Surely we are creating a better natural environment for them to inherit, than the one left for us by our forefathers?

However, what of the social environment?

With the lifelong job security a thing of the past, more working from home, communicating and being entertained electronically and the steady inexorable decline of religious, social and family structures and values, can that special South Derbyshire community spirit be maintained? Perhaps that's another story!

Councillor Mike Lauro
Chair, Leisure Services Committee
South Derbyshire District Council.

1900's Swadlincote High Street

In 1998 South Derbyshire Writers' Group launched the book 'Out of the Dark' bringing alive stories about the people and places in South Derbyshire from the people themselves. In 1999 the tape cassette 'Sounds like Swad' with author, narrator Graham Sellors gave us the voices and sounds.

Memories from the people who cut out our past from the earth in coal and clay. But what of the more recent past and the future? The new millennium?

Again we found it very difficult to choose what to include and what to leave out. We do hope you enjoy this collection of memories, selected to bring us through to today and on to the millennium.

'Into the Light 2000' starts with some of the stories that give a small glimpse at the courage, fortitude and humour of the war years. Then shows the determination to build on all the changes taking place both in our area and in the whole country.

The changes in the town due to the loss of the pits, pipes and most of the pottery works and shops that played such a great part in our lives. Salt Bros. when it closed the question was asked 'would Swad survive without Salts?' and had the store survived would it still use its Lamsom and Paragon catapult system to whiz the receipts and change from counter to cashier?

Years ago those in the area with any kind of artistic talent had little change of furthering it. The need to work, to help the family was of prime importance.

But now some of those who are blessed with those special gifts use their talent to give great pleasure. Painters, writers, musicians, artists of all kinds, our area has them all. Some in the Autumn of their years but all gaining and giving pleasure with their talents and passing them on to the young generation. Our young musicians, writers, artists and entertainers of the future.

The town of Swadlincote now has a fine new image and the area is changing again. But we know that the people of this area will go confidently on 'INTO THE LIGHT 2000'.

The South Derbyshire Writers' Group

chapter one
Through the War

Walls have ears

When aviation came into its own, a flying ace, named Alan Cobham, who became Sir Alan Cobham, got a few of his friends and a few planes together and formed what was known as 'Alan Cobham's Flying Circus.

As well as performing all sorts of stunts, they took passengers in the planes at five shillings (25p) a time. The aircraft back there were very flimsy and the cockpits open to the elements.

There was a story that went round of an old farmer who fancied a flight, but he didn't fancy paying the ten shillings for him and his wife and in true farmer fashion, he tried to get the price down a bit, until one of the pilots said. "I'll tell you what I'll do - I'll take you and your wife up and if you don't shout while we are flying, I won't charge you anything at all."

The farmer agreed, so off they went. The pilot took the plane through its routine. They looped the loop, went into a spin, dived almost vertical, yet the farmer and his wife made not one sound.

Eventually, when the plane landed, the pilot said to the farmer. "Well, I've got to hand it to you, you never made a sound. "I know," said the farmer, "But I nearly did a while back when the wife fell out!!"

In today's world of the 90's, we are used to seeing many different kinds of aircraft gracing our skies everyday. Microlights, gliders, helicopters, jets, planes that travel to exotic locations. The Concorde and who wouldn't like a trip on that. Even UFO's, well they've been around a long time really and nobody seems to be able to make up their mind what they are or where they come from. The skies are far more crowded than any of us realise...

However, if we go back a few years before the second world war, the only things that you would see flying in the heavens - with wings, would be the birds, for there were few planes of any sort about. On rare occasions, when an airplane passed overhead, everyone used to come out to have a look, especially if it was an airship - the R-88, R-100, or R-101. They were most impressive as they loomed out of the clouds, looking like an oversized cigar, powered by hydrogen gas and travelling at about 80 miles an hour.

But in my day, when I was a youngster living at Woodwards place, Coppice side, Swadlincote, there was an air display up at Woodville. It was a flying circus and they had bi-planes and the most spectacular thing was that the pilots were going to make a parachute jump and we'd never seen that before, but I was able to see it from my bedroom window and it was a great sight. One I will never forget.

Little did we know at the time, that planes of a different kind, sinister and death dealing, were about to fill the night skies and strike terror into the hearts of every man, woman and child.

There is no escape for Swadlincote town
Its lights have gone out, the town hall clock
wears a frown.
Shop windows that once were full and bright
are now covered with zinc and their wares out of sight.

Shouts of Take cover! echo down the street
followed by the sound of swiftly running feet.
Muffled voices and faces lined with fears,
heed the words -Beware! for from this day,
the walls have ears.

The homeguard is there to protect its town
and as their eyes search the sky
the clock still wears a frown.

What has happened to change this happy place
and given this clock a frown
upon its face.
Will things ever be as they were before
When the lights go back on, in every store.

Time goes by and still the clock waits
These sad and drear times for its townfolk it hates.
It longs for the days of laughter and song
When children played in its market place
all the day long.

All the mother's in the row had gathered to listen to Mary's wireless.

"Mam can I go out to play?" said five year old Beth.

"Hush Beth, Neville Chamberlain's on the wireless in a minute and your dad'll want to know what he said when he gets home from the Pit."

Mary drew the little girl to her, as the small gathering sat huddled around the crackling box, the wireless of the 30's

Put it up a bit Mary," said Rose. "I don't want to miss it." Mary leaned forward and as she did so, the little girl ran to the door; Mary chased after her and brought her back.

"But mam I want to go out and play."

"In a minute Beth! We've got to get your things ready first for school tomorrow." It's your first day there. In the momentary silence, Neville Chamberlain's voice was heard on the wireless "... and consequently," he said. "I have to tell you that this country is at war with Germany." The date was September 1939.

"There! Look what you've made me do Beth. I've missed the first bit."

"What did he say Mary?" said her Gran not hearing too well these days.

"He said we're at war Gran" and then Mary realised the import of what she'd just said and sat down at the table with a bump. "We're at war Gran," she said again, her voice faltering and her Gran began to cry. Mary had lost her Grandad in the first world war 1914-1918 and that was only twenty five years ago.

"It can't be happening again," said Gran, wiping her tears.

It's not real, is it Mary? said Rose her closest neighbour. "They won't want my young Harold to go will they?"

Mary put her hand on Rose's shoulder. They might Rose, he's a strapping big lad now, but don't worry; it won't be for long and he can look after himself. Come on, I'll make us all a nice cup of tea.

Mary turned away to put the kettle on the hob and her eyes filled with tears, she had her own worries about the future.

Even as the Munich Treaty was signed, German troops stood ready to attack and Britain had promised aid to Poland if they were attacked.

On September 1st, Germany invaded Poland. The British ultimatum to Germany to withdraw was ignored and by 11-O-clock Sunday 3rd, 1939, Neville

Before the war you could get anything. I mean, years ago they had pigs. Me mum used say. "There's nothing on a pig you can't eat, except its squeal. Mum used to love the trotters. But during the war they used go Roberts and Birches on Saturday morning and do the queueing. You could only have a quarter of this and a quarter of that.

Chamberlain said. I am sorry to have to tell you that consequently, we are at war with Germany. Minutes after this we heard the sirens wailing.

Many things followed. Windows were blacked out. Streets were blacked out. Road signs removed. We had double summertime as compensation.

Car drivers had a basic allowance for petrol, but later, had petrol coupons for essential travel.

We had to carry gas masks in boxes everywhere we went. Over 30 million were distributed.

In Jan 1940. Food rationing was introduced.

Butter	2oz	week per person.
Cooking fat	2oz	"
Sugar	8oz	"
Bacon	4oz	"
Cheese	2oz	"
Cheese	8oz	for miners
Tea	2oz	
Meat	1/2d worth	
Pkt dried eggs or 1 egg per fourtnight		
Sweets	2oz	

Bread was not rationed but the posters read Save bread, eat potatoes instead. Fish was not rationed.

I saw a queue at the butchers and when it was my turn, I asked. "Have you got any brains?" The butcher thought I was being rude and turned very red in the face, so I gave him a big smile.

In Swadlincote, we had a Restaurant at the foot of Alexandra Road and we could have a balanced meal, for a shilling - 5p. The lady in charge was Mrs Tilley.

THROUGH THE WAR • 15

1939-45 Second World War Ration books etc.

1990 Local display

*Me father had a suit made at Salts in the war
and turnups, you couldn't have turnups, cos
during the war there was a shortage of material you see,
so this gentleman at Salts
who knew how to get around that problem,
said to me father, he said.
"I'll tell you what to do Jo,
have them made longer,
and then come back
and we can do you turnups."*

*Soon after, he had this card
to say that the suit was done
and me mother went to Salts
and he said to me mother,
"Let's see, you're about the same
size as Jo, aren't you
and me mother said. "Yes"
and he says.
"Do you mind if I measure your inside leg?"
and when me mother came back, she said.
"That was my most embarrassing moment."*

Everyone was issued with a gas mask and at school we had to practise putting them on. They smelt of rubber and fitted close to the face, with a piece hanging down to breathe through. It looked like a small elephants trunk.

Small children had masks that looked like Mickey Mouse, or Donald Duck, it was to make them less frightening to wear and we had to carry the masks in a cardboard box on our shoulders, everywhere we went.

Many years after the war, I came across two gas masks each in their own box. They were in a shed of a house we bought for my mother. We had hoped that we could take them to a museum on war memorabilia, but not surprising, the boxes and masks disintegrated as we handled them; the rubber in the masks had perished.

When my wife used to do her washing, she'd put it in whitener (that's a blue bag) and hang the washing out, but ten minutes later when they were salt glazing in Swad, she'd have to bring it in and wash it all again 'cause it were covered in black spots.

Women were no longer considered just housewives. They were directed into munitions factories: On the buses, aircraft factories, in the armed services and on the land.WLA. In fact, they did any kind of work that men had done. Earning good money, the women began to like the independence it gave them.

I worked for a short time for the Ministry Of Food - Ration books. Then I worked full time for the Ministry Of Supply - Accounts. We all had identity cards. I've still got mine.

I remember just as the war started,
I'd be about fourteen then.
"Was that the first or the second world war Ron?"
"Eh ode on a bit Joan."
"As I were saying. I remember once,
when fish were a bit short
and Mrs Dodd kept fish shop,
top of Princess Street,
old Rusty went up to Arthur and said.
"Arthur, they've got no fish.
Mrs Dodd's got no fish."
"Aven't they," said Arthur,
so I said to him. "No Arthur, Mrs Dodd's got no fish,"
so off he went to the fish shop.
"Mrs Dodd," he said. "I want 30 fish and a pennorth of chips."
"Sorry Arthur, I've no fish today," said Mrs Dodd.
"I'll just take the pennorth then," said Arthur.

Most of the gardens were long years ago and there was plenty of room to plant vegetables, a lot of homes kept a pig, in fact some of them had two, because they weren't allowed any more in the war years. I can remember how busy the women would be after a pig was killed. They made pork pies, sausages, black puddings, faggots, chitterlings and then they would hang the sides of the bacon to be cured in the kitchen or living room and these were often referred to as - The best pictures in the house.

The days of people never locking their doors have gone and allotments and pigeon racing, in time may follow, but this is a story from the past to make you smile.

There was this man who always seemed to manage to have the first runner beans and broad beans and in the pub one night, he was bragging about it and said he was going to have bacon and beans for his supper, kept in the oven by his wife. While he was talking, one of the men in the pub, nipped out, while nobody was watching.

He hurried off to the man's home and when he got there, he could see the wife was out and so he quickly nipped in, fetched the plate out of the oven and with great relish, ate the man's supper. Then he nipped back to the pub.

When the other man got home, he was furious to find his supper had gone and blamed his wife and he didn't know who'd done it until many days after; what happened then is your guess as well as mine!

During the war I lived at Hill Street, Swadlincote, and I can remember the two land mines that were dropped. One landed on Wragg's yard and the other in Baker's Street. The first one broke all the windows in the street. The second in Baker Street took lives as well as homes. We saw the houses go up in the explosion. After that we all went to Wragg's air raid shelter until the all clear went.

We were rationed with food, but Swadlincote Market still operated, we went on Friday's and Saturday nights to see if we could buy something extra.

Mrs Davies used to fry chips in a kind of dustbin, frying them in the upturned lid. We brought a pennyworth in a newspaper.

I started work at fourteen in the blacksmiths shop at Cadley Hill Colliery, in November 1941. The shop had no natural light. The window having been painted out for the blackout.

This was the third winter of the war. Still, we were as well off for light as many of the shops in High street Swadlincote, which had corrugated iron windows with the words - BUSINESS AS USUAL painted on them. Davenports Wine shop will be remembered by many, having the words - 'OUR WINDOWS DID NOT STAND THE TEST, BUT YOU'LL FIND OUR SPIRITS STILL THE BEST' painted on the zincs.

Not an announcement that would create much excitement today is it, but in the dark years of the war, it was a beacon. With Europe almost entirely under the yoke of the nazis and with the seaways under their control, imports had almost dried up. Only fruit and vegetables grown in Britain were available and so supplies were seasonal.

The prospect of having tomatoes was exciting, as it relieved the monotomy of the diet. The national loaf had additional nutrients introduced to improve the diet, but unfortunately, the bread turned out to be a grey colour which didn't exactly stimulate ones appetite.

I remember that when my mother heard of the availability of tomatoes, she and Grandfather immediately, organised an expedition to the nursery (which is now Bretby Garden Centre) and from Wood Lane, Newhall to Bretby is a walk of about two miles each way. My brother had to go in his pushchair. When we got to Geary lane, we could see that we were not the only ones who had heard the news. The lane was crowded with people. Many of them - women with small children; whose destination was the same as ours.

Just beyond the present day Crematorium, on the left hand side and on a sharp right hand bend, a small footpath, known as 'Blind Sam's Gullet' cut through the woods and made a short cut to the nursery. Having arrived at our destination, we joined a very long queue and wondered whether we would obtain anything at all. We needn't have worried, because each person was allowed one pound and although I was only about 6 years old, I was allowed to claim a pound and so we returned home with 3 pounds of tomatoes.

They used to do the salt glazing at Wraggs when they were making pipes and when they were doing the glazing, you got the smoke up your nose and in your mouth, it were a bit choking.

Me dad used to tell me that when the war was on and we had to dig for victory, this man come round from the Ministry of Agriculture and me dad asked him. "Is there anything we can do to stop the salt glaze smoke from killing our stuff?" The man from the Ministry said. "What's Salt glazing?" he'd never heard of it. So me dad had to explain what it was, because on the allotments that me dad had got, it got the full blast of the smoke and stuff and it turned all the leaves on his cabbages and everything brown.

I was a shorthand typist working in Church Gresley when the war was declared. I ran in to my mother and gasped. "Mum we're at war!" My mother just looked at me and carried on cooking Sunday lunch, she thought I was pulling her leg. We were that kind of a family.

I used to walk to work three miles and back. Now, I had to carry a gas mask as well.

An underground shelter was dug outside the offices, but I don't remember going into it. I think most of us were fatalists - if your number was up that was it.

The blackout was severe and one night our chimney caught fire. There were sparks coming out the chimney pot. We thought the enemy planes would see it and blow the house up. It wasn't just our lives we had to worry about and we expected the ARP warden to turn up. We had to take the redhot cinders outside on dustpans and smother them with soil.

I married during the war and had my first child. Booklets were issued by firms like Woolworths. One showed us how to make do and mend. There were some great ideas for making existing clothes look like new ones.

We were able to get coupons for orange and blackcurrant juice for children and I remember constantly standing in queues for bananas.

In the towns and villages, Saturday dances were still being held, the war weary needed some form of diversion from the air raids.

The American troops and airmen arrived on the scene in 1942 and instead of a slow waltz across the floor, the girls were taught to jitter bug. The G.I's were always boasting. They were better paid and better dressed. The british soldiers shunned them, the good time girls adored them.

On the radio we had Vera Lynn - The Forces Sweetheart. Her favourites were - We'll Meet Again. The White Cliffs Of Dover and Its A Lovely Day Tomorrow. They were sentimental songs, but they helped fill the gap while our husbands were away.

I was born in Belmont Street Swadlincote, but when I was twelve months old we went to live at Rose Valley Newhall, opposite the 'The Jolly Collier.' It was a jolly pub. All the locals used to get there, including the boxing family - Bodells.

When I was a kid, I used to go up to my bedroom and leave the door open

I was eleven, a pupil of Belmont Street School in Swadlincote at the beginning of the war. In the first year the war had little effect on our daily lives until rationing became necessary. Until 1941, there was a basic range of Utility furniture for newly weds or those who got bombed out. Plywood and block board were mostly used and they had Units. A wardrobe was 8 units. A chair one unit. Parachute silk was much sought after for Wedding dresses.

and watch them all come out singing their heads off.

In 1940, I joined Newhall Homeguard and talk about 'Dad's Army' it hadn't got a thing on us - no way!

At first they gave us spikes for starters and the idea was that if a parachute came down, you'd stick him with the spike and send him back up again. Then they gave us some guns and you'd stick the bayonet on the end. We thought we were the cats whiskers, because we used to march around with these guns.

Our headquarters were down at Hawfields Brick and pipe works, in a shed and when the pit was going they tipped all the refuse and made a huge bank and we used be right on top.

My dad was a Corporal and he was a guide. One of the finest they'd had, because he used to take them round Bretby and always got em back in time for opening. It was hilarious really.

At the same time, I was in the Swadlincote air training corp, when it first started - the 1211. I was taking morse. I wanted to be an operation air gunner. I used go up to Baby Joyces place and take it there as well.

Later, I volunteered for the RAF and when the passing out came, I went in and they said. "Uhm Mr Rice." I said "Yes." and they said. "You've passed to be a pilot."

"But I don't want to be a pilot, I want to be a wireless operator air gunner."

"But we don't want a wireless operator air gunner."

"Well, I don't want to be a pilot," I said.

"Well, there's a new job just come out - the second pilot flight engineer."

"What's its price?" I said.

"Same price as a pilot," he replied. "Thirteen shillings and sixpence (67 p) a day. So I went home until they called me up.

When me dad handed me the letter, he said. "What the hell you've got to go for I don't know." He knew I was on a reserve job as a bricklayer at Hawfields, but I wanted to go to knock seven bells out of Gerry (Germans) well, you know how you are at nineteen, that is till I got there.

In 1943, we hadn't got a crew and in the mess, this guy came up to me and said. "Where do you come from?"

"Same place as you be the sound of your lingo," and he came from Derby and turned out to be a rear gunner.

The crew of the 'G'-George, Halifax HX349 of 158 Squadron in 1944.
Left to right: H. E. Rice (engineer),
H. Harmer (navigtor),
R. Higgins (mid-upper gunner),
J. Hitchman (pilot),
L. Fisher (wireless operator),
W. Tunstall (rear gunner) and
A. Pearson (bomb aimer).

24 October   Officer - Arthur Rice

"We want a flight engineer in our crew. How are you fixed." he said.

"Great!" I replied, so we shook hands and seven of us met, unfortunately, our first navigator got killed, but we stuck together all through.

My first trip was Berlin and the City. They knocked us about and I thought. "Well, if that's flyin' I'm a good mind to pack it in," but of course I had to do another thirty three missions after that.

The plane we had was a Halifax bomber, but first we used to fly G-George. We called it Goofy's Gift and on our fourteenth op, the wingo said. "I'm taking your kite to Nuremburg," and I said. "Well, that's a right thing," and he said. "Well, there's a new one coming in - F for Freddy, you'd better take that, which turned out to be Friday 13th, so we took it on its first trip to Nuremburg and they shot five or six of us down.

It was the toughest mission we did. It was supposed to be dense cloud over the target, but it wasn't, it was moonlight and I thought it were scarecrows coming up. Well, you see, Gerry used to send something up that burst, just like one of our aircraft going down, but they weren't coming from Gerry, they really were our aircraft. They simply burst into flames as they were dropping down. They never stood a chance. It was terrifying, but those German lads were doing a job same as we were. They were fighting for their country.

We never got shot down, but we had to lob away, in fact they used call us lobbers, Hitchman and crew, because nine times out of ten, we'd got to lob away, because of the petrol; we'd been shot up a bit you see.

On that Nuremburg raid, there were 600 of us went altogether and they shot all those down. We only just made it back to England 'cos we'd had a tank shot up. It was a bit hair-raising.

I courted my wife when I was sixteen or seventeen and we got engaged, but we said we'd never get married until I'd finished flying. Well, I finished in 1945 and we got married then. I was one of the lucky ones who came back.

Not one of the 6,178 Handly Page aircraft survived the peace, but in 1983, a project began, to rebuild the Mark three LV907 Halifax Bomber named Friday 13th. It completed 128 missions and served between 1944-5, with 158 Squadron at Lissett near Bridlinton East Yorks. The plane had every unlucky sign on it you could imagine, like upside down horseshoes and was christened Friday 13th.

Everyone in the crew, received either the DFM or DFC.

After the war, Friday 13th was on show in London and then they cut it up, but some years later, one of the fellows got to Scotland and he spotted this whole piece of an aircraft and it turned out to be the hull of 'Friday' being used as a chicken coop! The farmer said he could have it and it was taken back to Ellington, to the Yorkshire museum and they started rebuilding it in 1983.

1996, thirteen years later, on Friday 13th, it was pulled out of the hangover and we went to see it, all those who flew in it. It's wonderful to see it restored and in a museum.

The year was 1939 and dad was still in the territorials and me and mum and me sister Ruby, were there to see him. Dad had fixed us up in lodgings, so we could visit him at camp.

While we were there, war was declared on Germany and dad sent us home. A few days later, the Territorials from the Gresley group were billeted in the old tram sheds at Swadlincote.

Three weeks later, they were in France with the BEF and then they were all evacuated from Dunkirk. In between time we received a telegram saying dad was missing and believed killed, but thankfully it proved to be wrong and he came home to us.

He was discharged with shell shock, but we were glad to have him home.

Two land mines were dropped on Baker Street Swadlincote and it brought the full row of houses down. My brothers went up to try and dig some of them out and I knew a lot of them. It did extensive damage all over the area, even some of Salts shop windows were cracked and blown out

Baker Street was sealed off and it made it difficult for me, because my future husband wanted to come up to Weston Street to see if I was all right, but he wasn't allowed up because all the area was actually roped off.

I remember Violet Brown, she was holding a baby and they got her out.

When my future husband and I went to Leo Murray's to give notice of marriage, a lot of people were there for the death certificate of those they had lost.

THROUGH THE WAR • 25

The Hull of 'Friday" used as a Chicken Coop!

1996 'Friday 13th' Rebuilt at Yorkshire

Those who were killed in Baker Street, were Joseph Bull and his eleven year old daughter Betty, who died in hospital. The other two victims, a man and his wife were discovered among the wreckage next day while demolition work was still in progress.

Among those injured were Mollie Bull the eighteen year old daughter of one of the dead and Annie Brookes aged eighty. A number of others were treated for shock; yet there were some amazing escapes.

One man had put his wife and two daughters in a neighbours air raid shelter before he went on emergency duty and shortly afterwards the bombs had done their damage in the street.

May 1940 - Germany invaded Holland, Belgium, Luxembourg. British and French troops were sent into Belgium.
May 10th - Neville Chamberlain resigned as Prime Minister. Winston Churchill became Prime Minister.
May 28th - Belgium surrendered and evacuation of French and British troops began.

One thing was certain - evacuate the troops, head for Dunkirk, the only way out. Thousands of French and British troops were swarming into Dunkirk. Long lines of weary men waded into the sea from beaches, waiting for boats and ships to take them back across the channel to England. Small boats were needed to get the men off the beaches. The Armada of little ships began to make their way from Ramsgate to Dunkirk. Excursion boats, yachts, life boats, barges, anything that could float. It was estimated that 340,000 men were taken to England, French as well as British.

On August 1940, the battle of Britain began. Germany needed to have control of the air before invading England. All night raids were made on London and they set Dockland alight.

A second wave of bombers followed. They were attacked by Hurricanes and Spitfires, which broke up their formation, but the raids went on.

September 15th was named Battle of Britain Day, Churchill's message to the country - Never in the field of human conflict was so much owed by so many to so few.

When I went Monkey Parading, it was during the war and it was all blackout. Pitch black in Swad. There was no shops lit up. We used to just stand in a doorway, talking to a lad, but the police come along. "Come on now, move out this doorway. We never thought of doing any damage and we didn't even go snogging, 'cause it was all so innocent in them days.

1940's Newhall Homeguard

With the bombings on London, there were not enough shelters for them so they moved into the tube stations with blankets and sandwiches. They felt safer down there.

During this time rumours abounded - German spies. Fifth columnists, were said to be busy among the population. Lord Haw Haw, our own traitor, was having a field day over the radio. My Aunt Sylvia shook her fist at the radio thinking he could hear her from down the speakers. She shouted back at him - "We arn't starving I've just killed a pig."

In 1942, the war had been going on
three years.
I was thirteen and the ARP, that's
Air Raid Precaution, asked us children
to pretend to be casualties in a mock
air raid.
We had to lie on the floor in certain
parts of Swadlincote.
I was at the end of Swad, where Needham's
shop was and we all had cards across our
fronts, to say what was wrong with us and
I could see them giving refreshments and
taking them off, in mock ambulances,
(carts and vans)
and giving them rides here and there to
Schools - mock hospitals,
and being bandaged up.
So, I never got no refreshment and
no lifts anywhere.
They just left me there.
They kept coming and looking on my card,
and I was so disappointed, I didn't get a
drink, or a biscuit.
Well! There's no point in giving anybody
anything that's dead is there!
I just got up in the end,
and went home,
and told me mum how disappointed I was.

The poachers were not only interested in feeding their own families. They were a special breed. They were the kindest of men and had a wonderful knowledge of nature. A boy would be taken on his first poaching expedition when he was about ten years old and could run fast enough to escape the gamekeeper.

Once they were used to the moonlight raids, it seemed to get into their blood and they became good poachers for life.

They all had nicknames like: Pussey - Nutman - Chick and Nimble. That's just to mention a few.

On suitable nights, they'd be off to the nearby Bretby woods and they'd come back with rabbits, hares and pheasants, which they sold very cheaply or gave away. Often one would find a rabbit or a hare outside the back door early in the morning, dropped off by one of the returning poachers.

They even had a code. No poacher considered it stealing to take the animals and birds, which in their opinion were provided by nature. On the other hand, none of them would take anything which they considered was rightly the property of someone else and if any of them broke the code, they were ostracised by all the other poachers.

One morning, I went with Matt Thompson to old Nimble's cottage. We knocked on the door and Nimble looked through the window, before letting us into the kitchen. The floor was covered with rabbits and Matt said. "Me mother's sent me to see if I could 'ave a rabbit please." "Aye, course you can lad. Pick a couple of good uns up off the floor and tek em 'ome to ya mam and tell her old Nimble's sent em.

Nutman, was the postman by day and his duty consisted of delivering the mail twice a day from Newhall to Bretby village. He did this on his bike, or walked if he had too much to carry on his bike.

In this way he had a wonderful opportunity to observe the signs which would lead to a bit of poaching at night. For instance, he noted the exact place in a tree where pheasants roosted and he knew that they always roost in the same place.

Nutman also knew every trout stream and he was an expert trout tickler. He took me and showed me how to do it one night.

He lay on the bank of the stream and shone his bulls eye lantern on the edge of the water and I watched in amazement as the trout came to the side of the

The Thorp family, from Midway. Peter, Margaret and their parents, ran out of their home and lay on the lawn, because they thought the bombs were dropping in Midway, but it turned out to be the night they were dropped in a field near Orme's shop, just below the Admiral Rodney at Hartshorne. The following day, Peter went to see the damage. He then said that he'd heard Lord Haw Haw of (Germany Calling) on the radio, jokingly say that he had sunk the Admiral Rodney at Hartshorne's dock yard. (Lord Haw Haw had visited the Admiral Rodney before the war.

stream, then all he did was tickle the underside of the fish and he just lifted it out of the water. It was an easy way to go fishing.

The oldest poacher was Baggy, he was over eighty and still going strong. One night though, he fell and broke his leg. He literally crawled home and to everyones surprise, his leg healed and he carried on poaching until he was eighty nine.

We came to Netherseal, a small village on the Derbyshire, Leicestershire border in 1941. The first batch of the evacuees came from London/Southend region. A girl, named Rene came to live next door. Every day we had to travel to the only School in the village and with all the evacuees there it caused a lot of overcrowding.

In the evenings, mother would pack me a few sandwiches and off I would go into the nearby fields and pick the bright orange rose hips. These would be sent away to be made into rose hip syrup. Blackberries would be gathered by the basketful, to be made into jam. Most of the school children at that time did all the collecting.

Planes terrified me. In my ignorance I was sure that every enemy aircraft was piloted by Hitler, he was the bogeyman mixing a child's world of fantasy into the adult complex world of grim reality.

One beautiful sunny day in September 1942, it was Sunday dinner time and the sirens went. We saw one lone German plane go over Rickman's corner, Mount Pleasant. It machine gunned Donisthorpe Pit chimney and also dropped a bomb before proceeding towards Derby where it was shot down by big bertha. (gun)

The morning was clear. there was frost in the air,
So was death, already winging away from his lair,
But we did not know as we talked, Jack and I.

I suppose we were an ill-matched pair,
He tall and thin, I short and square
Yet we both had a liking for music and art
And seldon if ever, we strayed far apart.

We had been to a concert the previous night
Now we eagerly talked of the music and might
Of the conductor Barbarolli on New Year's Eve.

The last piece played was Auld Lang Syne,
The audience rose, clasped hands and sang,
Even now I remember your hand in mine,
Should Auld Aquaintance and how it rang.

Suddenly, upon our talk flew agony on green wings,
With a trail of black exhaust smoke through the sky,
Many fingered death rattled and then was still,
In the following silence I heard you sigh.

I saw the smile fade from your eye
My trembling lips formed a cry,
I called your name, but you never spoke
With your shattered body in a leather coat.

I saw your eyes change and look afar
As though you searched for an unseen star,
Your breath was blood and as it came
I wanted you to speak my name.

But a stronger voice was calling you
And without a sound your soul passed through,
For you had flown the dark and smelled the cloud,
Now you lay dead with bloody lamb's wool tatters
For a shroud.

When the war started,
me dad went in the Home Guard,
but it wasn't called the
Homeguard then,
they had an arm band
LDV (Local Defence Volunteer)
Me mother said it was
LOOK - DUCK - and Vanish.

So, when the Germans come
to the low countries to scare us,
and after Dunkirk, they were thinking
they were going to come all the way
and invade England.
The Home Guards were looking for
parachutists and of course,
me dad used stand on top
of Castle nob there
with a beanstick in his hand,
and they called 'em
the Home Guard after that.

I think it's rather strange
that me dad should stand there,
with only a beanstick in his hand,
against the might of the
German Wehrmacht (German Army)
when they come through the low countries.
What could he have done with
only a beanstick. I suppose, it's
laughable now, but by gum
it were real in those days.
Everybody had to pull together

Sent to the country

In reading the actual experiences of the three evacuees who kindly sent in their stories to 'INTO THE LIGHT 2000' you will see that each story compliments the others and you will read their innermost thoughts.

If you put yourselves in their shoes and relive those experiences as you read them, you will perhaps come to the same conclusion as I did - How brave ALL the children were...

Sixty years ago, on August 31st 1939, I was 11 years old and on that day, my parents told me that there was a practice evacuation of children, in case there should be a war, that practice was the next day, Friday 1st September.

I was taken to Saltley station Birmingham and put on a train with other boys aged 10-13 years. "It's only for a few days, don't worry," my mother said. An hour later, the train stopped at a place called Swadlincote and being a shy lad, the next few hours were a bit frightening. We were taken to a place known as the Rink and I remember feeling very alone and vulnerable. I didn't know many of the other boys, because I was in the process of changing schools.

On arrival at the Rink, we were given a white china mug with the following inscription. S.D.U.D.C. Birmingham Evacuees Received into Swadlincote District. Autumn 1939. (I still have that mug. It's on display in my lounge) Anyway, there I stood at the Rink, alone and forlorn, when a very tall lady looked at me and she said to the lady with her, I think I can manage another one," so there were 3 of us, all 11 years old and I don't remember how we got there, but we ended up at a farm in Midway.

Later that day, we sat listening to the radio and heard the Prime Minister saying, war had been declared. I realised then that the practice evacuation had been for real.

I had a wonderful time on that farm. What an education we had! One of the ponies called Billy, pulled the milk float, delivering the milk round to Midway and Newhall. On Fridays, we would go into Swad to the bakery to collect all the week's sweepings up for pig swill. I used to get pocket money for helping out and on occasion, would buy a model aeroplane kit from Swad, they only cost a shilling (5p)

I well remember the Sunday School Anniversaries and being on the platform and of course we had to have new clothes, so off to the big shop in Swad we went. Mrs S was a good soprano and often supported the Chapels.

So much happened in those 3 years, I have promised myself, I must have a last look at where I had a wonderful time and say thank you Swad. I count myself very lucky to have had the experience.

Before Brenda Weber was evacuated to Hartshorne in 1944, we had at least two other evacuees. A young boy named Monty Barnet from Southend and then we had a man come to stay with us. Where he came from I've no idea. He wasn't English. His name was Julius and he was quite happy living with us, us, until the villagers began to suspect he might be a spy, so he discreetly moved away. We traced him after the war and found that he was living with his sister, in Nottingham and he made us very welcome. I can always remember we had kippers for tea with him.

As the war progressed, London was bombed daily and suffered much damage. Many lifelong friendships grew from those days. We thought of Brenda as part of our own family and I felt as if we'd always been together. We were such talkers. We must have driven my parents to distraction sometimes, because we used to talk through most of the night.

When we ran out of energy while playing in the fields, we used to lie on the grass looking at the clouds, using our childish imagination to form pictures out of them - as most children do.

It's a shame that as we grow older, we tend to stifle our imagination just because wer'e expected to act as adults. But as all adults know, we remain children at heart.

We could hardly tell the war was going on where we lived in the country. Now and again, the sirens went and mum made us get under the table. It was just a game to us. A few bombs were dropped, but we were too young to realise what it was all about.

As the war neared its end, the evacuees began to drift back home to the City.

Even before war was declared, plans were laid to evacuate children from cities to safe areas in the country.
I remember meeting our train load of children at Swadlincote station, each one carrying a gas mask and either a small case or a paper carrier - no plastic bags then.
We had two sisters Beryl and Irene. They had nothing except the clothes they stood up it.

We returned Brenda to her parents. It was only then as we climbed the steps to her large three storey home, that I realised just how hard it must have been for her to live with us in our tiny two up and two down cottage, with an outside loo and no bathroom. No wonder she said that nothing was familiar.

While there, my parents and myself took the opportunity to spend a few days in London. On the Saturday evening, while our parents were out, Brenda and I were in a downstairs room, sharing a very large metal bunk bed.

We had a tiny candle in a metal box for light (the end of the war had not yet been declared) and the window was still curtained with thick material. No light could seep through.

Suddenly, there was a heavy explosion, the room vibrated and the door was blown off its hinges; we were sprayed with glass, yet amazingly enough escaped with just a few small cuts.

On the following day we went to see what had happened. An unexploded bomb had gone off and flattened two streets not far away. We had been in the line of the blast and we all thought how ironical it was, that Brenda had been sent to the country for safety and there at the very close of the war we both could have been killed, through being in the wrong place at the wrong time!

When the end of the war was finally declared, we again travelled to London to share in the celebrations. Thousands of people were dancing in the streets. Buckingham Palace was surrounded by happy Londoners and there were people splashing about in the fountains and shouting from the tops of lampposts they had climbed.

The first I remember about evacuation was when my friend Brenda Bibby told me that she and her sister Margaret were going to the country because of the doodlebugs. I thought it sounded a lovely idea. I asked my mum about it and the next thing I knew, I was off with lots of other children from school.

My mum packed my case. She had a list to go by and one of the items was a liberty boddice, which I had never worn before.

I had a label with my name on my coat and I carried my favourite doll and possibly a gas mask since we'd had practise at school how to put them on.

We got on a train at Hornsey station where we said goodbye to our parents and then just before we got on to another train at St. Pancras, to take us to Derby, we had a check up by a nurse. She looked at our eyes, nails, hair etc. and also she pulled out the elastic in the top of my knickers to check down there. I suppose it was to make sure I was a girl! Everyone must have had it done. I giggled about it in embarrassment. Well, I was only seven years old.

When we reached Derby, we got on a bus. It was a long journey and the bus driver got lost. We were going down narrow lanes, instead of the main road and to me it felt that the bus filled the whole road. I looked out of the window on one side and then I ran to the other side to see if there was enough room for the bus to get through.Eventually, very tired, we arrived at Hartshorne village.

We went into the school assembly room and we must have looked a sorry sight. The chairs were all round the sides of the room and at one end was a table with someone sitting there. People kept coming in and going out again. I had no idea what was going on. It looked as though the people were choosing which child they wanted, by just going round looking at us.

I remember the room gradually emptying and I wasn't picked. Mr friends said. "Let's go into the playground to the lavatory and then we won't get picked by anyone and we can go home again. So, we went outside, played about and hid until someone came and took us back in the room.

Brenda and Margaret Bibby went off soon after and I was left with hardly anyone else there at all. It did begin to feel stange then, being all alone. Then a lady took me by the hand, so I was pleased to be wanted.

We went outside together and walked down a country lane, She said she was taking me to her home in Repton road and I was to call her Auntie Dolly. There were women standing at their gates, smiling and looking at me, but I just felt lonely and unhappy and began to cry.

Auntie Dolly (Mrs Parry) had a daughter named Joan, two years older than me and she had a dog named Judy. I cried most of the time, because there was nothing that was familiar. Joan was friendly and Judy barked at me, but I was too unhappy to be very sociable. I stroked Judy a lot, it gave me something to do in those first strange moments.

When it was nearly bedtime, I had a biscuit called a wagon wheel (not the chocolate kind, but a shortbread) It seemed a a very big biscuit and I nibbled

When I was a junior, I used to like fishing. The first time I went, was to the top pond at Bretby. My mother came with me that day and we hadn't been there long when the fishing licence bailiff came along and, yes, I did have a permit. I soon felt a fish bite and the float went right under, gradually, I hauled the catch towards the waters edge. My mum was panicking. "What shall we do when you land the fish?" To be honest I wasn't sure myself and we were the only people there. Just a couple of feet away from the waters edge, the fish emerged and then the hook broke and the fish lived to swim another day. we both gave a sigh of relief. Next time I went, there were more experienced anglers with me and I caught a tench. Someone helped me to take the hook out and photographed me and we then returned the fish back to the pond.

away at the edges in between my tears.

Then a man came in with a black face and his white eyes were peeping out. He had red lips and a great big smile. I had never seen a 'black man' before and it was such a shock that I stopped crying. This was Uncle Jack Parry and he'd just come home from the coal mine (Rawdon) I had a job to understand him as he spoke very broad Derbyshire.

The bedroom were Joan and I slept was very small, whereas my home in London was Victorian with large rooms, five bedrooms, a bathroom and upstairs and downstairs a W.C. So I was horrified that I would have to go outside to the lavatory. I didn't like that at all and was scared because of spiders and other creepy crawlies and one day, there was even a frog!

The milkman (the one who delivered the milk in bottles) used to come in and get his money out of a drawer in the sideboard if Auntie Dolly was out. She obviously didn't lock the front door (unheard of in London, even at that time)

There was a field at the bottom of the garden with cows in. I was frightened because I hadn't seen cows before. and I didn't know what cowpats were. We spent many happy hours in that lovely field, looking for tiddlers in the stream and we often went for walks in the fields, blackberrying.

I don't ever remember it raining. It was always nice weather, except for winter. It was very cold and I had to wear woollen stockings - and they were buttoned on to that awful liberty boddice. The snow drifts were up to the hedges and we couldn't go to school until the men came and cleared a pathway for us.

The three of us were evacuated, my two sisters - Joan, Mary and myself. It was in May 1944. Brenda Bibby, Brenda Weber, Freddy Winters and his sister Brenda all came with us.

I wasn't frightened of leaving home, just excited. I remember going to the station with our name tags and gas masks. We went from Hornsey station to Kings Cross and then to Derby. It was such a long day and when we got to Derby, we got on this old bus or coach and it seemed ages going through the country lanes to Hartshorne, which is only a twenty minute ride to Swadlincote, the nearest town. I remember all of us standing in the school hall, waiting to be picked out by a family.

My sister Joan, has sad memories, as she wasn't as lucky as us. She doesn't remember the names of the people she stayed with, because she was only there a few weeks. All she remembers is being given chips cooked in margarine. Joan Wasn't allowed to go to the Grammar school like she did in Hornsey and she developed a terrible ear infection; my mum came over and took her back home.

Mary and myself had very happy memories. We lived with Mr and Mrs Dolman and were treated like their own children. Alan Dolman was blond and seemed to be the same age as me. Jeff Dolman was a lot older. He went to Grammar school and used to spend his spare time playing the piano in their front room.

We went to Sunday school and I had a bible given to me on the Anniversary day, where everybody sang on platforms. I still have it.

On one occasion at Church, the organ stopped playing, because Freddy Baldwin had stopped pumping.

It seemed that all ages of children were in one classroom.

At Christmas, my mum sent a parcel, but I can only remember the spinning top. I still have it and won't ever get rid of it.

Mary, my sister, broke her arm in 1945 and my mum came over and seeing her after what seemed ages, I wanted to go home, but as soon as I was home, I wanted to go back to Hartshorne, but of course I couldn't. My mum still kept in touch with Mrs Dolman and spent several holidays there.

My mum brought back from the potteries TG Green, several items. I had a fruit dish and bread and butter plate with the green dots on.

At school we had singing lessons and I can remember learning 'Good Morrow Gossip Joan,' and one morning when the vicar came, he picked me to say 'The Lord's Prayer,' I knew it pretty well, having been to a Church school in London, but I got a bit mixed up at the end and missed a bit out. I was so embarrassed, but I don't think many children nowadays would even know what the 'Lord's Prayer' is, let alone say it in front of a class!

One day, I had a bad accident. I fell off a bike that belonged to a big boy who lived nearby. I had to tell Auntie Dolly, because it wouldn't stop bleeding and it hurt and I shouldn't have been on it anyway. The neighbour, Mrs

Malpass, came to look at it and they decided it needed stitches. I was scared and had no idea what it involved and it didn't sound very nice.

The doctor lived in Woodville and Auntie Dolly and I had to walk all the way there, which was very painful (the buses didn't run very often) Looking back now, the doctor's surgery was primitive. It was a wooden building next to his house. It was dark and only had one window and shelves with bottles and things on them.

I sat down and Auntie Dolly held my leg while the doctor pushed wire through the wound to bind it together (I'm cringing now while I write this) It hurt so much. I had no anaesthetic that I remember and I've had a fear of doctor's ever since.

When we went to Swad on the bus, to the shops, we passed some mines and slagheaps. It seemed rather gloomy along that stretch of road.

I was amazed at having a bath in a tin bath in front of the fire. I didn't think it was decent to be in the living room having a bath and I felt shy about going in it and I never did get used to having to go outside to the lavatory.

At the back door was a water butt and we had our hair washed in the rain water from this, because rain water is softer than tap water (said Uncle Jack) though I must admit I wasn't too keen on the insects that floated on the top, but of course they were strained off before use.

I expect we fell out over silly little things like children do, but it's lovely we've kept in contact and have this special link. I am proud to have been an evacuee and delighted that I was lucky enough to be chosen to live with Joan and her parents.

As children, we were never frightened of the bombs and at home we used to sleep under an old wooden kitchen dresser when the bombing raids were on.

My dad was in the homeguard and every time I see Dad's Army on the telly, it reminds me of him, because he was the same build as Captain Mainwaring and dad always took his duty so seriously.

The railings were taken from our front garden.

We didn't have much damage, except the windows were blown out, but they were soon repaired and when the war ended, everyone in the road decorated their houses and there were street parties.

I was almost five when the war was declared. We were taken with my mother to Huntingdon, but nothing much happened for the first six weeks and because my eldest sister and father missed us, my mother brought us home.

Not long after we came home, the bombing started. Sometimes, we would stay in bed with the covers over our head and sometimes we would get dressed and crouch under the solid kitchen table. Some people had shelters in the garden, but we didn't.

Hornsey was a real target for the Germans. The train ran through Hornsey from Kings Cross to Scotland. So it was the main line up North and they wanted to stop supplies.

As time went by, the bombing got worse. No lights were allowed after dark. We had black out blinds at the window and very dull bulbs. Several times our windows were blown out, but luckily our road wasn't bombed.

The bombs got bigger and I think it was 1944, that we were sent home from school with a letter, asking us if we would like to be evacuated. I remember we were given very little notice and I had no idea where we were going.

I can remember waving goodbye to my mother on the station. I was with my youngest sister Tricia and an older sister Joan. It was dark when we arrived in Hartshorne. Tricia and I were the last ones to be housed and it was pouring with rain as we walked up from the school with Mrs Dolman who lived at Church Street.

One of my school friends, Barbara Smith, stayed in a house on the left hand side of the road, that went to Woodville.

Life in then country was very different. I have very fond memories of going to the farm up the lane to collect the milk. There, Annie and her father would let us in the farm yard to see the cows.

I remember waiting for a calf to be born and called it Blackie. - Years later, when I visited them, Annie's father told me he never got rid of her, because she reminded him of me.

On Saturday mornings, I would walk round there and we would take the nanny goat for a walk on a long bit of rope.

I thought it very strange at school that children of all ages were in the same class.

Mr and Mrs Dolman were very kind to us but strict. I enjoyed Mrs Dolman's cooking, but couldn't understand why we had to eat batter pudding with jam on it before we had our dinner.

We only had batter pudding with roast beef or sausage toad. Tricia liked Mrs Dolman's thick gravy and wanted to marry Alan, so she could have thick gravy forever.

We enjoyed the freedom of living in the country. Right opposite, was the village recreation ground and it was while playing there that I slipped and broke my arm. After that my mother came to visit and when Tricia saw my mother, she wanted to go home, so my mother took us both back with her. It wasn't long after that though, that the war ended in 1945.

It was then time for celebration. Every street in London had their own party. All the houses in the road were decorated and God knows where all the food came from, as it was still rationed.

Looking back, people never moaned about life. While there was a war on everybody just accepted it.

About five years ago we took our two eldest grandchildren to Kent for a holiday. That year, they had just opened up all the rooms in the Cliffs of Dover museum. They had all little exhibition rooms, telling you all about the war. This is where it was all planned to bring all the soldiers back from France. There was also a film of this and we are sure we saw my husband's father in it. The grandchildren were very interested in seeing all the old equipment. Phones, Ration books and gas Masks etc. It really took us back in time.

From the land mine explosion in Baker Street, it blew my window in and the glass covered my bed. I was under the bedclothes at the time. The next day I went to see the crater and found some scrap for souvenirs. It was a night to remember.
Aug. 1940

In the early days of the war,
I packed a big biscuit tin with
tins of various food, like tinned meat
and fruit, then with a saw I made a
big hole in the pantry floor.
I put the biscuit tin in it and
re-placed the boards and re-covered
the lino.
To this day, I can't remember taking
the tin out and often wonder if the
new owners ever did.

In 1998, I plucked up courage and rang
the current owners of the house and
enquired if they had ever looked under
the floor boards in the pantry.
I think they must have thought I was
potty and said they hadn't and there
was a cabinet of some sort standing there
now.
But perhaps the previous owners to them
had looked under the floor boards, although,
they would not have had a reason for doing
so,
except perhaps, noticing the piece of floor
board that looked different to the rest.

Well, I guess I'll never know for sure now,
will I!

Cloak and dagger stuff

Eileen Harvey of Newhall was working for the Ministry of Food in Swadlincote on D-Day. She had no idea that her husband was somewhere in France as a unit member of the Allied Planning Staff who masterminded 'Operation Overlord'

Doug Harvey, who died in the 80's had been a company director at Rawdon Ltd in Moira before his army service. When he came home on leave he said he was going away, but don't ask him where - he couldn't say.

Doug, a sergeant, went over on HMS Hilary and landed with the 3rd Canadian Infantry Division on Juno beach near Courseulles.

He was 'mentioned in dispatches' and later awarded the Belgian Croir de Guerre in another cloak and dagger job inside occupied Belgian.

They were 'sealed in' well before D Day at operational headquarters where Doug took an oath of 'silence.' He learned all information by heart.

On D-Day, Doug landed on a dangerous stretch of Juno beach and what he experienced there was with him always and one of the unit Ivan Thomas, became his life long friend.

Gladys has lived in the Swadlincote area for a very long time and we've often chatted together, but it wasn't until we began talking about the war years that I realised what a traumatic time Gladys had gone through when she was young.

It was one of the worst war time tragedies that could ever have taken place. On April 16th 1945, six people died when a light aircraft went out of control and crashed on to a row of terraced houses in Stafford street, Burton on Trent.

Gladys was twenty three at the time and she lost her mother, Aunt, two cousins and a baby nephew. She told me what had happened in her own faltering words -

It was a Monday morning, I was working at Marley Tile as a welder, doing a man's job, but of course the women in the war were all doing men's jobs and all I had on was a boiler suit over the top of my other clothes when I was asked to go to the office. The Minister from my local church, which was Sydney street Methodist, said. "I've got some bad news Gladys; your mother's missing."

1939 - 45 Eileen & Doug Harvey. Newhall

I remember wondering what he meant. My mother always did her washing on Mondays. She would have been working in the kitchen, filling the boiler with water and lighting the fire to boil the clothes.

We had a large mangle that turned a long wheel to put clothes through and there was the dolly pegs and posha and all that sort of thing, so mother would be too busy to go missing. Then the Minister told me about this plane that had crashed in Stafford street. the houses had collapsed and they couldn't find my mother.

I rushed back home on my bicycle with him, but I was devastated and don't recall anything that was said to me. I suppose I must have been in shock.

By the time we got there, they'd found the bodies, but I still remember the awful smell of burning; it stayed in my nose for a long time. Two of my cousins that died, their husbands were both away in the forces.

A week or so later, one of the workmen found a little ring box and he asked me if it was mine. It had two rings in it. My father's Signet ring and my mother's Engagement ring. I still wear them both often. He couldn't have found anything that meant more to me than that.

Eventually an officer from the RAF came to see me and I had to make a list of everything that had been in the house and the cost. I had to guess some of it.

In the end I received about a £140 compensation, which was a lot of money in those days, but £100 of that went on mum's funeral.

All I had left was the boiler suit I was wearing that dreadful day, so I had to go to a welfare office and they gave me £9 to kit myself out in new clothes, which I had to repay.

The date this all happened was about a fortnight or three weeks before the end of the war, which was May 8th 1945 and at that time British and American troops were winning the war in Europe. There was an air of optimism among the townfolk, fuelled by the belief that long years of conflict would soon be over.

Even more bitter then, was the tragedy to befall my mother and relatives who were killed. They would be chatting over a cup of tea in the back kitchen of their terraced home, the younger ones no doubt speculating on the return of their husbands from the war, when this light aircraft plummeted from the sky above them and all four, along with the neighbour and the planes pilot - were dead.

On VE DAY we had street parties. We had races for the children and adults too. I came first in a hundred yards race and got a box of Beecham's pills for a prize.

An inquest held a week later, heard from witnesses who had watched the aircraft perform three or four horizontal rolls, as if the pilot was stunting, then a-wing dipped and the plane had spiralled down, hitting the houses in a sheet of orange flame.

Popular belief was that an american was showing off to his young lady but the pilot in fact was an englishman. All this was reported in the Burton Mail. No doubt details of the crash lurk in the depths of official record offices; but at the time there was more concern for the people inside the homes.

Some were saved in a remarkable rescue by a sixteen year old girl, who had dashed into one of the houses and helped out two small children; but the firemen at the scene found only desolation and death.

I've never been able to forget it, but I don't blame anyone. Whatever the airman was doing was silly, but I can't help wishing that, had there not been a war at that time, this man would not have been in a plane in that situation and I think it was partly the fault of the war. I just wished my mother had lived a bit longer, to a bit of an easier life, like we have now. She'd been through some very hard times.

The neighbours were very kind and helpful, they managed to rescue a few belongings from the front of my house. Among them were my bible and methodist hymn book, which I still treasure and they both mean a lot to me in my life as a christian.

Those who lost their lives along-with the pilot in the plane were Mrs Ivy Gor, aged 29 of 53, Stafford Street, Burton on Trent. Mrs Elizabeth Bantam age 80. Mrs Edith Baker age 25. Brian Baker, age 20 months of 55, Stafford Street and my mother, Mrs Agnes Emily Jones, age 59, of 57, Stafford Street, Burton on Trent.

An inquest held by the Borough s deputy Coroner, Mr F.Long, recorded verdicts of accidental death.

In 1944, Hitler let loose his secret weapon - The V1 pilotless flying bomb, released from coastal launching pads in France. When the fuel was used up, the buzz bomb fell from the sky and nothing could stop it. They were called 'Doodlebugs.'

In September 1944, a more powerful weapon was launched from Holland.

1999 Gladys Adams nee Jones

The V2. It also was pilotless and steered by a magic eye mechanism.

The Danish Resistance Movement attacked the factory and blew it up, putting an end to the V2.

In July 1945, the Red Army marched into Berlin.
Hitler died on May 1st 1945. Age 56.
On May 7th, Germany surrendered.
VE Day. Victory in Europe was celebrated on May 8th 1945.

In the evening there were bonfires, singing and bands playing late into the night.

Street parties were held the next day. Tables were set up outside and people brought out their reserve stock - tins of meat and fruit. There were sandwiches, baked cakes and fizzy drinks.

In due time the men came out of the army and returned home in their new demob suits. Some children knew very little about their fathers. As one child put it. "Mummy, that's your husband at the door."

When my husband went to war, Michael was just a baby and every night I used to lift him up to a large photograph and tell him. "That's your dad."

Years later, when Michael was about five, he came running in from the living room,clasping a box and a piece of newspaper. "My dad's a hero," he shouted. "I found this medal in the desk!" It was the Belgium Croix de Guerre - awarded for outstanding service to Belgium.

Records of Servicemen Photographed at the War Memorial at 11am Thursday June 11th 1998.

SGT Jack Hassell.
114 LAR Regt RA.
Served North Ireland Belfast. Trained in Scotland on landing craft for D Day.
One of the first twenty to land on (Juno Beach) in Normandy, with the Canadians. In Arnam in Holland, also in Belgium Antwerp port had a lot of 'BUZZ BOMBS.'
Went into Germany for 12 months, demobbed June 1946

Brian Laxton.
Joined 1943.
Served in Black Watch at Perth Dumfries and Lockerbie. Sent to France in 1944 and transferred from Black Watch to 1/5 Welsh Regiment of the 53rd Welsh Division 2nd Army General Dempsey, until May 6th. 1945, was in Hamburg. Hostilities ceased on 8th May. 1/5 Welsh Regiment Disbanded 1946 and was transferred to the 6th Armoured Division in Berlin.
Spent the best part of 2 years in Kingston Jamaica.
Demobbed 1948.

Eric Johnstone.
LAC,
Joined the RAF 1940-1946.
Posted to Egypt 1941-1944.
Served with the Desert Air Force.
Attached to No3 Squadron Royal Australian Air Force for 12 months.

Arthur Rice's mum was concerned and asked him. "When your plane has been hit and you have to bail out, how do you keep the plane level before you jump?"
Well mum, said Arthur. "We leave George in charge," His mum replied, even more concerned. "But how does George get out?" Arthur laughed. His mum wasn't aware that George was the automatic pilot!

A.E.Rice DFM 158 Squadron.
Joined the RAF in June 1942, passed for Air Crew in 1943
as F/E. Started flying Halifax Bombers in 1943.
Flew 34 Operations by June 1944, all my Crew were decorated
in 1945. 5DFC and 2 DFM. I got the DFM. I was commissioned in
1944 and Demobbed in 1947 as FL/LT
I also flew in the famous Halifax called Friday the 13th.
This Bomber did 128 operations. We took it on its first operation to Nuremburg. They shot down 96 Aircraft that night, the heaviest losses the RAF ever had. Later they said that 110 were lost, and 700 men were lost. It was shown in London; then later, they cut it up. Now it has been rebuilt at Yorkshire Air museum and took 13 years to rebuild.

1998 J Hassell, B Laxton, E Johnstone, A Rice

I went on holiday to Domasadala in northern Italy about fifteen years ago and I had a very surprising encounter there.

I was having a meal at my Hotel and kept being badgered by the waiter who was particularly inquisitive. He asked endless questions and when he got to asking me "And where do you come from in England sir." I replied snootily. "Nowhere you've ever heard of. It's a little market town called Swadlincote," he instantly cried out with some enthusiasm "Ah! TIME THE AVENGER."

I couldn't believe it, I was even more shocked to discover that he'd been a prisoner of war at Shellbrook. Ashby de la Zouch and had worked on farms all around the area and had made regular visits to Swad!

1945 Roland Toon - Luftwaffe Barracks Taken over at 'Evere'

Only the wind cries when the charred bodies no longer moan along the dust. Dry burnt clouds flee from the holocaust. Stricken trees stand bare, a grave for Spring, Yet it does no matter For the birds no longer perch and sing. But hobble mute and blinded on the sterile earth. Dead fish float white in the boiling pool And the blackened angler seared to his stool Dehydrates in the scorching gust.

Fingers once human scrabble in the dirt Then try to find the mouth. Let conscience crawl on its naked belly, So it should. We cannot go back, Yet we trod the step that brought us here. We pressed the button and released this fear.

SUPREME HEADQUARTERS ALLIED EXPEDITIONARY FORCE

Soldiers, Sailors and Airmen of the Allied Expeditionary Force!

You are about to embark upon the Great Crusade, toward which we have striven these many months. The eyes of the world are upon you. The hopes and prayers of liberty-loving people everywhere march with you. In company with our brave Allies and brothers-in-arms on other Fronts, you will bring about the destruction of the German war machine, the elimination of Nazi tyranny over the oppressed peoples of Europe, and security for ourselves in a free world.

Your task will not be an easy one. Your enemy is well trained, well equipped and battle-hardened. He will fight savagely.

But this is the year 1944! Much has happened since the Nazi triumphs of 1940-41. The United Nations have inflicted upon the Germans great defeats, in open battle, man-to-man. Our air offensive has seriously reduced their strength in the air and their capacity to wage war on the ground. Our Home Fronts have given us an overwhelming superiority in weapons and munitions of war, and placed at our disposal great reserves of trained fighting men. The tide has turned! The free men of the world are marching together to Victory!

I have full confidence in your courage, devotion to duty and skill in battle. We will accept nothing less than full Victory!

Good Luck! And let us all beseech the blessing of Almighty God upon this great and noble undertaking.

Dwight D. Eisenhower

Letter from SUPREME HEADQUARTERS ALLIED EXPEDITIONARY FORCE.

*At last peace returned
to the villages and towns.
In Swadlincote the lights
went on in the shops,
and the sound of laughter
filled the delph.
Instead of the muffled voices
of fear,
we heard the cries of
market vendors
selling their wares.
'Apples a pound, pears!' and
in the High Street, the
shopkeepers with their
big beaming smiles
took the strips of tape
from off the windows.
We knew then that
the war was
over.*

*The clock can now
look down on its town.
The smile on its face
replaces the frown.
The cloak of austerity
falls to the floor.
The town picks itself up and
becomes as before -
A happy bustling place.*

1990's A Rice and R Pointon remember

chapter two
Exciting Years!

The Bone Setters

I was what they called in those days,
'Granny reared'
Families looked after their own
without outside help of the sort
you get nowadays.
My Grandma was a little
grey-haired woman who was
terribly lame.
She had a large family, so
I was surrounded with Aunties and Uncles.

On odd times when funds allowed,
Grandma would send to Simpsons,
the butchers,
at the top of Stanhope Road, and buy
a sheep's head for about four pence,
and into the pot it went.
I used to come running home from School
and say. "What's for dinner Grandma?"
She would turn from the pot
on the stove and say,
"Mountain pecker my lad."

When I looked into the pot,
there, rising and falling,
as it bubbled among the vegetables,
with its bright green teeth
and sad eyes,
and its tongue hanging out,
was the sheep's head.
A meal fit for any Prince.

Straight after the war, none of the shirts had collars on. They were all loose collars. You could buy a stiff collar from Salt's which had been starched. One day a young woman came in and asked for a soft man's collar size 15.

Another day, a lady came in and said. "I want a pair of trousers for me husband," and I said. "What size do you want madam," and she said. "I really don't know. He's a bit like you," so I said. "Well I take a 34inch waist and 31" leg," and she says. "Well he takes a size 9 shoe, will that help!"

There were no nylons straight after the war. Artificial silk stockings were 5d a pair and if the girls couldn't afford them, they'd paint their legs and draw a black line up the back to make it look like a seam.

We did have a horse and cart delivery and we had to pull the dray. The horse was called Peggy.

We'd deliver anything to the householder, even if it was only a brush stale. One day, a lady rang and said. "Will you slip into Colliers the butchers and get half a pound of liver, put it in a parcel, and I'll pay the driver for it."

We'd got alarms on the shops and I used to take the keys home with me at night and probably at 1-O-clock in a morning the police would ring and ask me to go down to the shop, because somebody had broken in. When I got there, a policeman was waiting for me. "You go ahead and stop the alarm," he said. So I did. Then he said. "You go first, in front of me," and I wondered why he said that - he was the policeman, so I asked him why. "It'd be a bit difficult," he replied, "if someone jumped out on us from behind a counter, wouldn't it." I agreed. Anyhow, the burglars had gone out the back way.

I went home and got back in bed, but an hour later, I was up again, the alarms had gone off, but this time, the heavy rain had set them off.

The next day, I told Mr Salt. "I was up twice during the night and come down to the shop," but all he said was "Aye," he says. "It's a nuisance losing your sleep," but of course, he didn't pay me for coming down.

We measured for suits at Salts, but a company in Nottingham made them for us and we could get them within two weeks. I found that nobody in this area had got a tape measure. People used to come in with a piece of string or elastic, or even tape and they'd say. "I want a pair of trousers made, for me husband and this is the length he wants it. We only used charge a shilling (5p) for alterations.

*I 'ad a pair of brown shoes from Salts,
an' I've still got 'em.
This young woman come to serve me
an' I picked this pair of brown en's.
They were all leather,
an' er says.
"They're three pounds, ten shillings,"
an' then er says,
"We've got some black en's an' all John,
an' they're Clarkes. They're good shoes,"
So I says. "How much are they? an' er says,
"They're three pounds ten shilling," so
I tried 'em on, an' I 'ad two pairs
for seven pounds! an' I'n bin
married thirty one or two years,
somat like that, an' the woman who
served me, er's bin at Salts years, cos
it's thonly job er's ever 'ad.*

*I'n still got them shoes and
they're still as good as
the day I bought em, other than
the leather's started crack.
I always put stick on soles on,
and when they'd worn, I
took em off an' put some more on.
I've 'ad the brown en's 'eeled,
but I don't think the black 'ens
'av bin 'eeled.*

I know this is true, because the woman come in, sat down and tode us about it.

Erd lost er wedding ring and er said to my son. "Have you got a metal detector?" which he had, an' er says. "Will you come an' find me wedding ring, I'n lost it."

Well, he went all over the garden an' he never found this wedding ring, so they gave it up as a bad job.

Anyway, after Salts had finished and they were cleaning the drawers out, cos er worked in women's lingerie room (underwear) and when they were cleaning the drawer out, they found er wedding ring and that were years after.

I was born during the Great War and I think those of my generation were probably the last to see and take part in village life.

During the years between the two wars, changes began to take place; slowly at first and then gaining in momentum. In the late 30's until after the second world war, most of the traditional way of life had disappeared. To illustrate. No planning had gone into the layout of the houses, which could be described as higgledy-piggledy. It was often said that when the horses that were pulling a load of bricks, became tired, the driver tipped the bricks off the cart and there the house was built, yet to me, this very lack of planning gave the place a fascination of its own.

Paths and right of ways were to be found in the most unusual places and some of the rights of way were established a hundred years ago, when coal was taken to Derby by pack horses, with a bag of coal being hung on each side of the horse. Twenty or thirty horses formed a team and naturally, these teams took the shortest route. In the village of Newhall, the George Inn was built directly on one of the rights of way and every year, Bill Wells, the local barber, would demand the right to walk through the public and private rooms of the George Inn.

He entered by the front door and left by the back door. This he did to keep the right of way open and it became an expected ritual for Bill to walk through the house once a year, getting the landlord to sign the book to the effect that the right of way was still open.

EXCITING YEARS! • 59

Bonfire night was a bit different years ago. A day or so earlier, one of the local Collieries (Nadins) would deliver ten tons of coal, to a field. They gave it free of charge for the annual celebrations. Early in the morning of Nov 5th, old Baggy the poacher, would light the fire and build it up during the day, so that when night came, there was a huge coal fire giving off terrific heat.

Meantime, a number of small fires had been built and as everyone gathered in the field, so the celebrations of Guy Faulkes night began, with home made fireworks being set off.

The general merriment was increased by eating bloaters and potatoes, which had been roasted at smaller fires and drinking mulled ale.

The ale was poured into a copper muller and cone shaped vessel, holding about one gallon. To this was added about one dozen (12) raw eggs and a generous supply of ginger. The muller was inserted into the fire, point first and the contents stirred continuously, until the brew was considered hot.

Mulled ale has a taste of its own and when fortified with a few glasses of the brew, even on the coldest night, quite a few men wouldn't be fit to go to work the following day.

We never used to travel far from home, yet somehow life seemed to be exciting with nothing to be bored about.

Occasionally, a farmer would have a fire in his hayrick yard. This was excitement indeed. The fire engine had to come from Swadlincote. But first of all, the four horses had to be brought in from the fields, harnessed to the engine and the firemen themselves had to make their way from home to the fire station. These were all part time volunteers. There were no full time firemen in those days.

I remember one fire at Abbotts farm. Eventually, the fire engine arrived with its bell ringing and clanging.

Immediately, the engine drew into the farmyard, Jody Parker came out of the house and shouted. "Come in and have a drink me lads before you begin." So into the house trooped all the firemen and sat drinking strong ale for an hour or two, before attending the fire. Needless to say, the fire had destroyed the hayrick yard and almost burned itself out before the firemen came outside again, by which time they were in no fit state to care what happened to the hayrick.

Summer was a time of hard work. Jack Barratt had a large family and when there was little work at the Pit, he'd get his scythe out when the hay was ready and many a time he'd mow and mow hour after hour without straightening his back and he'd mow an area for eight hours and when there was a moon, he'd mow through the night, just to earn a bit of something for his family.

Walking along Hearthcote Road seventy years ago, with a small group of boys and girls from Stanhope Road on one of the walks we used to take, it seemed a long way for us, because we walked slowly; taking everything in with our young and eager eyes. We chatted away together, for although we did this walk many times, there was always something different to see. Every now and again one of us would run ahead and put our ear to the telephone pole and tell the rest of the party that someone was on the phone, but of course it was only the wind in the wires making music down the pole.

We passed by some rough uncared for fields and there was a large pond in the far corner of the last one, by the side of the railway line. It was always called Boardmans pond. We walked on and came to an unused pipe yard with the down draught kilns still standing.

Hall and Boardmans stood a little further along and even that looked old and neglected, but still chuffing away turning coal.

At the top of a lane near the Pit stood a Lanashire boiler, long enough for all of us to put our ears to. We all stood in line and listened to the thump, thump, of the boiler feed pumps. Yes they are turning coal one would say and we all nodded in agreement.

We would stand against the railings and watch the boiler cooling water spray tank, with its many jets and if it was a sunny day there would be rainbows in the spray. We all thought it was beautiful and magic.

Not far from there stood the mill pond. The mill long gone, but even today, if one knows where to look, the pond is there close to the road.

Passing down from the mill pond stood an old farm. It was so old and nothing like one sees in this day and age. All the farm buildings seemed to lean on each other looking as if one gave way the whole lot would come crashing down into a pile of tired bricks.

The whole purpose of this, is to take us down to the Isolation Hospital, which stood in a lane on the right hand side going towards Catchems Inn.

It was a galvanised iron building painted green. The lane was signposted ISOLATION HOSPITAL - STRICTLY NO ADMITTANCE.

When I was a small boy the doctors were struggling with a maze of illnesses that for most of the time it was only with the help of God that they managed to get some cures.

Diseases like: Pneumonia. Consumption. Rheumatic fever. Measles. Chicken pox, all of which can be prevented today, by being vaccinated against the disease.

When there was an outbreak of disease which looked like spreading rapidly, the patients were moved to the green painted isolation hospital to be nursed until they got well or died.

Houses with spreadable disease, used to put the patient, usually a child, into the bedroom and hang a sheet soaked with disinfectant over the bedroom door.

If you had any library books the council collected them and they were fumigated before being returned to the library.

Doctors have improved in knowledge and technical skill and are slowly winning the battle against illnesses that killed 60 years ago. Now with drugs, needles and research, the green galvanised hut is a long distant memory.

The Writers and contributors who helped to make 'OUT OF THE DARK' an overwhelming success, felt that 'INTO THE LIGHT 2000' should give some mention of the Doctors who have served this community for decades.

I remember the pictures hanging in the passageway of the new surgery and health centre at Darklands Road, beginning with one of the founders, Doctor Parkhill. Of course, I cannot remember him personally, but my father in law, Phillip Orme, spoke of him from when he was a small boy in a family of nine children. He said he could remember him doing his rounds on horseback and later, with motor cycle and sidecar.

The two doctors of my early childhood, were Cochrane and Moir, in practice at Belmont Street. The house is now a dental surgery.

I often wonder, now I am older, how doctors lived in my childhood, because hardly anyone had any money to pay them and if they had, it was pennies and sixpences, but for many of the patients, it was free.

Doctor Jim Camac, had his surgery as part of a large house, opposite the war memorial at Church Gresley, with Doctor Julius Summ and was later joined by John Camac, after the war, that was Jim Camac's son.

I remember Doctor Summ well, because of his cars. The first one being a tiny Fiat 500 and later, a Jowett Javelin, which could really move. My mind is a little hazy to when the surgery moved to Swadlincote, opposite the park memorial gates, now a Barber's shop.

There was Doctor Robertson, big and bluff. He always used to say. "They call me the old folks doctor." Ian and Cleaver Keenan, Jim and John Camac and then, this very young man, Doctor Goodacre and I hope he doesn't mind me saying this, but I can see him now, sitting at his desk with his book open on pills and practises. Now substituted by the computer. How time flies!

Then in 1991, the new surgery was opened in Darklands Road. It was designed by Brian Ambrose, an architect, with whom the practice has had a long association. The building was well laid out, with a treatment room and Sister in attendance, to give injections and what have you.

I said previously, how time flies, now Doctor Goodacre is 'Senior' at the head of a good team of doctors, including a lady doctor for the shy.

You are old Father William, the young man said.
And your hair is exceedingly white.
Yet you incessantly stand on your head.
Do you think at your age it is right?
In my youth said the sage.
As I mentioned before, I kept all my
limbs very supple.
By the use of this ointment, one shilling the box,
Allow me to sell you a couple.

I must say that I have written this from memory and if I have omitted anyone, I am sorry. I have liked the quote from 'you know who' since I was a small child and could not resist ending with it. I thought Doctor Goodacre would like the quote.

As a young girl of ten, I had to walk to Castle Gresley, to visit the doctor. Doctor Ord did not often come to our house and Gran paid two pence (old money) each week for any medicines we needed.

There were three large glass containers on a shelf with medicines in. One brown, one green, one white and whatever your illness, you had your medicine from one of these.

We didn't have pain killers in those days. If I had earache, gran would boil an onion; cut it up and fold it in a big bandage, made from a worn out vest. This was tied over the ear and under the chin. Actually, it was less painful to suffer the earache, than to have a hot onion poultice tied to your head.

After 1939, I lived in Swadlincote which bordered on Newhall. The doctor's surgery was but a hundred yards away. The waiting room had wooden benches and there were three steps down to the consulting room. If the light was switched off, it was quite dark down the steps and one day our friend Frank, made a visit to the doctor and stumbled down the steps.

The doctor was quite apprehensive. "Oh dear!" he said. "Are you hurt young man? You must be feeling very unsteady on your feet. I think you should have some time off from work. Come and sit down while I write a certificate for you." Frank wasn't in a position to argue. He could only say thank you and he came home with his certificate. Actually, he'd only gone to ask the doctor to call and see his mother! NOT to be put 'on the club'

Special people.

A doctor of some repute was Dr Cochrayne. He was very stern and straight to the point. Dr Frazer Senior was my doctor in the early part of 1939. He came to Newhall from Scotland and was a friend of Dr Moir, who also came from Scotland. He lived and had his Surgery at Brook House in Swadlincote, which is now a Dental Surgery.

Doctor Ord used to be one of the family doctors of Castle Gresley. He used to do his rounds in a horse and trap, but later, had a car and Mr Ison used to drive him round then.

Doctor Ord's surgery was a single storey building, reached by a drive lined with trees.

Inside the surgery, a corner of the waiting room was partitioned off and served as a dispensary. The shelves on the walls held large bottles full of different coloured liquids and in one corner was a wash basin. Doctor Ord's daughter was the dispenser and we could watch her through the hatch as she

1991 Swadlincote Surgery, Darklands Roads

This is an old surgery joke. It came from a time when such as Doctor Ord would stitch a wound if it needed it, or any minor surgery. Nowadays they use those butterfly things that they stick over an open wound, and it holds it together until it begins to mend. Amazing what the body can do isn't it. Anyway, this man went to see his doctor, and when he came out, his wife who was waiting for him, thought he looked a bit crest-fallen. "What's the matter Bill?" she asked. "Well," replied Bill. "The doctor's put me on some pills, and he says I've got to tek em for the rest of me life." His wife smiled at him. "That's nowt," she said. "Lots of folk have to do that." "I know," said Bill. "but he's only given me fourteen!"

poured liquids, either brown, white, or pink, into a glass bottle, through a funnel and then topped up with water and sealed with a cork. The dosage was marked clearly on the side of the bottle.

There was no appointment system in those days. There were benches to sit on and patients just had to wait to see the doctor. As each one went in, everybody kept moving up, so we all knew when it was our turn.

Some of the surgeries had a coal fire and often it was a long wait, so everybody talked about the latest village gossip and compared symptoms. There was always one person who'd joke about illness and tell a tale or two of some sort to cheer everyone up, like this for instance - A man leaned over to a youth sitting beside him and said. "Wot's up wi yo then ma mon?" The youth described his symptoms and the man replied. "That sounds just like me Uncle Ben and doctor Ord was 'is doctor." "Is he better now then?" said the youth. "Oh no," replied the joker. "Way buried 'im las' wick," and he'd wink at everybody in the surgery.

As Doctor Ord grew older, a young doctor from Scotland, named Doctor Rose, joined him in the practice. He was young, good looking and over 6 feet tall and he also spoke with a Scottish accent that was difficult to understand. It must have been nigh on impossible for Doctor Rose to understand what the South Derbyshire patients were saying. Think of someone going to the surgery and saying. "Arve got peens in mi nays doctor and I cudna goo ta slape las' nate, an' ar was buzzed fer wok this mornin'." The Scottish doctor would have a job sorting that one out.

Doctor Rose was popular, but unfortunately, he had to go back to Scotland, due to ill health.

Bill Wells, from Newhall, was not only a Barber, he was a keen fisherman, having once caught a giant pike in Bretby ponds. He was also a bone setter and many of the older people would get Bill to set a broken arm, rather than go to the doctors. He always kept his shop open until 11-O-clock on a Saturday night, until after the pubs had closed and was always kept busy - shaving men in readiness for Sunday morning.

Often, when they'd had an evening in the pub, any man who had a toothache, would ask Bill to draw the offending tooth and without any more a do, Bill would extract it for him - with anaesthetic of course. He was also proficient in lancing boils and removing cysts. The modern doctor would be horrified at all this, but I never heard of any of Bill's patients not recovering.

Just after the war was over, I was about ten or eleven and someone came to the school to exam all the childrens' eyes. I suppose it was to see who needed glasses etc,. I hadn't realised at that time that I didn't use my right eye much, this showed up in the examination. We had to read those cards which had big letters on and when they tested my right eye, I could only vaguely see the top letter which was a Z.

After a few more tests they discovered the reason. I'd had measles and unfortunately, it had destroyed some of the tissue in my right eye, of course I had to wear corrective glasses after that, which never made any difference, but on that particular day, the lady put drops in my eyes which gave me blurred vision and I had great difficulty getting home.

When my mum suggested we go to the Cinema at Swadlincote, I didn't like to say that I couldn't see properly, also, I didn't want to miss a trip to the silver screen.

While waiting for the bus, I climbed the stile at the Rodney at Hartshorne, to watch the bus come from Ticknall, down the hills and round by Screwmill. When it reached Screwmill; childlike, I tried to beat the bus to the bus stop.

I reached out for the post to climb down - missed - and fell on to the pavement. There was a loud crack! and my arm immediately began to swell. The bus arrived. It was full. We got on and I had to stand all the way to Swadlincote which was a twenty minute ride, in absolute agony.

You can't get your beer on tick these days, so they tell me, but when the mines were still operating, you could get it on the slate. It used to hang on the wall behind the bar and if a man was out of cash, the landlord would let him have a few drinks. The debt was chalked up on the slate at the side of the man's name.

When eventually, the debt was paid off, the record of it would be rubbed off the slate. Hence the old village boast - I've got a clean slate!

When we got off the bus, I was sick and looked as white as a sheet. Mum decided to take me to the nearest doctor, which was in Church street. I never forgave him for cutting the sleeve out of my best brown velvet dress, but he had no choice; my arm was so swollen.

Instead of sending me straight to the hospital, he sent me home by taxi and that was when we discovered that the glass tray on my dressing table had shattered; most of it was all over the bedroom floor. Neither of us was surprised, because the old house that we lived in, had an unseen presence that lived there with us and it showed how it felt when either I got injured, or my dad, hence the broken glass.

Dad worked at the Pit at Rawdon and each time he was injured, the pictures on the wall always fell down, just before they brought him home on a stretcher. Anyway, we were used to things happening like that, so mum just cleaned the glass up and said nothing.

The following day, the same taxi took me to the hospital in New street, Burton on Trent and after a number of xrays I was led down a corridor to the operating theatre. I lay on a sort of table covered with a sheet and someone said, as they put a thing over my face. "Breathe deeply and count to one hundred."

What a strange experience it was. I managed to count to four, but by then I felt like a balloon, as if I was floating up into the air. When I came round from the anaesthetic I was in a hospital bed and my arm which was fractured in three places, was in a sling.

Mum and dad came to see me later that day and they had brought me some comics to read, but my vision was still blurred, so I had to wait a few more hours before it wore off and I could read them. In fact, I was beginning to think that it would never wear off.

I was in hospital for three weeks and it was a long time before I could use the arm again. When they took the sling off, my arm had set in a bent position, but it gradually straightened itself out. It's never been as reliable as the other one though.

Years ago we used to have thick peasouper fogs, a lot of snow and frost that lasted many weeks. I was thirteen at the time when the snow came in 1947 - a year that nobody forgets. I lived down Repton road Hartshorne, in a place called Jail Yard.

The neighbours and friends had dug a narrow path up to the school and in some places, the snow was ten feet high each side of the road.

Come Saturday afternoon, the snow hadn't budged and my mum was used to taking me to the Cinema at Swadlincote. She didn't want to miss it if she could help it and neither did I, so although it was very cold, when it was time for the Trent bus to come from Derby, we set off with half a dozen of the neighbours, also from Jail Yard.

As we stood at the bus-stop, near the Admiral Rodney, we could usually see the buses coming over the hills; but this particular day, the double decker we were hoping to catch, was travelling very slow and eventually it stopped altogether. "It must be stuck in the snow," said mum.

We stood there for ages watching it, expecting someone to come along and dig it out; but in the end, mum had to admit, "The bus can't get, it'll have to stay there until the snow thaws. Come on, we may as well go back home." We were all very disappointed and the kids especially from the yard were moaning about it not being fair that we couldn't go.

We all trudged back to Jail Yard, but when we reached the entry, mum said. "How about us all walking it the bottom way, up Sandcliffe road and down into Swadlincote. It's not far." That cheered the kids up no end and we were all dressed for the weather, so we set off.

At first it wasn't so bad, but once we'd left the Repton road, the lanes that were so familiar to us in normal conditions, looked like a vast snowy wilderness. There were no footprints we could follow.

We'd been walking for sometime with our heads down, because of the wind and when somebody suddenly said. "Where's all the hedges gone?" we stopped and mum looked around for a landmark and realised that we had walked over the TOPS of the hedges and we were heading over the fields.

"It's no good," she said, out of breath. "It's far too dangerous. We'd better go back," so we struggled all the way back home again, muttering to ourselves, thinking about the film we'd missed, but the kids by then were so

EXCITING YEARS! • 69

1947 Snow covered local road from that year

tired that they didn't care any more.

When we got back, we couldn't just settle by the fire and switch the television on, because nobody had got one. Televisions weren't about until 1950. We had to get the games or the jigsaws out for entertainment, which was a bit of a let down from watching Stuart Granger or James Mason do their stuff on the big screen.

We'd had weeks of snow and ice 1957 and I worked at Bullen's in Ashby at the time. One morning I caught the bus from Swad to Ashby as usual just after eight. It was quite full, but we only got as far as the hill leading out of Swad. The bus had really struggled to get to the top of the hill, which at that time was very steep, but at the top, the vehicle in front, almost stalled and as soon as the driver of the bus put his foot on the brakes, the bus started to slide backwards down the hill and no matter what the driver did, he couldn't stop it sliding. It was frightening.

I was sitting on a side seat at the back of the bus and as it continued to slide backwards down the steep hill, most of the girls who worked at Green's, jumped off, while I sat it out.

The bus continued its slide right down into Swad and came to a standstill outside Woolworths, without any mishap.

The driver however, not to be outdone by the ice, took another run at the hill and this time, he made it and continued on through Woodville, but he had to give up at the Smisby turn; he couldn't get any further and we had to get off and walk single file, through the enormous snow drifts.

We used to have terrible thick fog years ago and one day, I finished work at 4pm, got off the bus at Frederick Street and went to my mother's in Granville Street for a late dinner. Then I decided, because it was still foggy, to walk to Stanhope road in Swad where I lived, instead of catching another bus as usual.

I walked down Swad road as far as Woodhouse Junction and crossed over to continue down Hill Street, but I heard traffic coming behind me - and it sounded much too close for comfort.

When I turned round to look, there was this bus right behind me. When the driver saw me in his headlights, he stopped dead and I told him he was

One lady was reminded of when she was a child and she used to play her mother up something awful - crying for nothing, but, her mother would always box her ears and say. "Theer y'ar, that's gen ya summat ta bawl for."

EXCITING YEARS! • 71

1930 Hill Street, Swadlincote

travelling on the wrong side of the road, so I guided him back to the other side and walked in front of the bus, all the way down the steep hill; I had a torch with me and I kept guiding him back each time he veered over to the wrong side.

Eventually, when we got to the bottom of Hill Street and the bus turned right to go up Church Street; behind him were three double deckers and two lorries.

In the later years, after the first world war, there used to be motor vehicles that would haul the coal, some of the blacksmiths then became mechanics and so you had garages.

We had our own car built in Swad - PARAMOUNT. There were only thirteen produced in Swadlincote, before it was moved to Leighton Buzzard, but certainly, there was a group of people in this area who built what in those days was quite something - A MOTOR CAR.

Swad's Pride

In January 1991, the South Derbyshire Writers Group put up a Display of old photographs of Swadlincote and the following day, I took my husband, Bob, into the library to see it. We were both engrossed in the photographs, when we spotted one of the very old shaped police cars. It just looked as though it had come out of one of the films of the Keystone Cops and for some reason it reminded me of the fact that Swadlincote, at one time, had its own Car.

"Did it look like that? I asked Bob.

"No," he said, laughing. "Not that old. I saw it once in Elliot and Dilkes Showroom. It was a sports car."

I sighed and thought, 'I wish I knew more about it.' Suddenly, a voice behind me said. "I remember the car," I turned round, to see a tall smiling elderly man looking at me. He also must have been looking at the photographs on display and it seemed as if he'd read my thoughts.

He looked at me. "I remember the car," he said. "It was quite something in those days, for it wasn't long after the second world war when it was built and it was said to be before its time. But if you want to write about it, I can go one better for you. I know one of the men who actually worked on it."

My eyes must have lit up, because I was honestly thinking that they must all have gone by now.

"I'll tell you where he lives," said the smiling man," and he did. I was so surprised by what had happened, that I didn't get the smiling man's name, but I do hope that he is able to read this, then he'll know how grateful I am to him.

Ray Evans, the man who actually worked on the car, is in his 70's and he laughed when I said. "Can you tell me anything about the car made in Swad!"

"Just a minute," he said. "It was a long time ago. I have difficulty remembering dates and names these days. It's been written about in the papers," he said, "and it's been on the telly, "cause there's one still running about."

"Yes," I replied, " but I was too young to be interested in cars then, I haven't seen any of that, so I'm depending on you."

"Let's see now," he said, and his old grey matter began to delve into the past.

"Well!" he said. "About 1950, a man named Billy Hudson had a dream. He wanted to build a car, but he knew that he would need others to help him if he was to turn his dream into reality. The war hadn't long been over you see, so there wasn't a lot of money about for a project as big as that."

"Billy came to Bob Kenny's garage, to see a man named Sam Underwood, who was the foreman, and Billy told him what he'd got in mind. Sam must have liked what he'd heard, for he became Billy's partner in the project of building Swad's own car - 'PARAMOUNT'

I was working for Bob Kenny at that time and they asked me to join the team. There was about a dozen of us altogether and they were all skillful men.

The car was a 4 seater sports car with a Ford 10 engine. The body was aluminium on an ash frame. Everything on it was hand built, including the upholstery and the car had a metallic finish.

We began building the Paramount car in a workshop at Woodville, but then we moved to several other places, Melbourne and Swadlincote. (The hard topped car was made at Melbourne) and before finally moving on to Leighton Buzzard, we had produced 13 cars. It was an exciting time.

Comments

The Paramount was a tremendous achievement and I am sure that as Swadlincote's history continues to unfold, there will be other surprises along the way.

EXCITING YEARS! • 75

Above - 1950s Left to right: Sam Underwood, T. Wright, Ray Evans, R. Saunt, B. Waldron, C. Cave, C. Atkins, H. Hopkins, B. Barrett, Billy Hudson. Paramount Car 363 NU.

Left - 1998 Ray Evans, worker on the Paramount car

In 1949, Walter Jones, Harvey and Co Ltd, of Swadlincote, made arrangements for supplies of televisions to come in steadily, so that they could spread the work out, and have as many customers as possible fixed up for the opening programmes.

We were quite used to listening to records and the radio, especially, radio Luxembourg. I used to run home from the bus-stop, after spending an evening dancing at the Rink in Swad on a Saturday night, just so I could finish the night off by listening to radio Luxembourg - it was a magic programme. But when the telvisions first came in, there are no words to express how we all felt, as we stood there with mouths and eyes wide open, crowded round a black and white television with a nine inch screen, that one of the neighbours had bought on tick.

We were looking at the test card which never moved until the programme came on (televisions took a while to warm up in those days). Then we stood, watching these tiny figures moving round this tiny screen and not only moving, but speaking as well. We were all rooted to the spot, absolutely fascinated, and then suddenly, the picture began to roll and everybody started to moan until somebody twiddled with the knobs and the rolling stopped.

The neighbour had to put up with most of us every night, until our own parents, not to be outdone, went out and bought a television on tick as well.

We were hooked by the box in the corner. We gradually stopped going to the pictures, television had taken over. It was easier to sit in a comfortable arm chair watching the box with a packet of crisps (blue salt packet in the bottom) than risk either missing the bus home or not being able to get on.

Like most things we ended up taking the television for granted, as if it had always been there. The screens got bigger and the casings more streamlined and it wasn't long before the picture was in colour and all the early teething problems were ironed out and now they're all geared up for the new wide screen televisions and lots more channels...

They say that what you don't have you don't miss, but I'm not so sure about that. If we hadn't had television, when we did, we would never have been able to witness the walk on the moon.

On July 20th 1969, more than 350 million people sat before their television sets, waiting to see the first step on the moon, and at 10.45 that night, we heard Neil Armstrong's voice. "The hatch is coming open," and a few minutes later, he was at the top of the ladder and we saw him descend to the surface of the moon. Everyone must have held their breath as he reached the foot of the ladder and took his first step on the lunar soil. He then uttered the sentence that will always be remembered world wide. "That's one small step for a man and one giant leap for mankind."

Can you remember your first television in the early 50's. I got married in 1953 and after building our own home and furnishing it with the essentials, we didn't have anything left for such luxuries as a television set. Still, we were quite content with our modern type radio, which also played records, the old 78's. But then we discovered we lived opposite a man who liked to tinker about with radios and televisions, in a shed at the bottom of his garden; we could tell he had some kind of hobby in that line, because of the noise in the evenings, which turned out to be almost every evening.

Anyway, one day to our surprise, he came over and asked if we'd like a television and before we could say - sorry we can't afford one, he said. "I've got a television you can have for £3.10s.0d. It's a nice walnut type case, with a nine inch screen. It'll be a nice start for you."

We jumped at the offer, knowing that if it went wrong, Gordan, would only have to nip over the road to mend it. Actually, the licence cost more than the television.

I used to love Sunday afternoon, when my Uncle Bill Parry used to visit us. He cycled all the way from Stone row in Moira (it's no longer there now) to Hartshorne.

Uncle Bill's bike was like nothing I'd ever seen, before or since. Instead of handlebars, it had a wheel, with gears on and a seat with a back to it. He was a cycling enthusiast of his day. He wore a brown leather zipped jacket that was waist length, a cloth cap, cycle clips on the bottom of his trousers and he smoked a pipe while he cycled. He also had a tandem and when he took Aunt Bessie for a ride on the back, she wore a long grey coat, hat to match and three quarter length boots that looked as if they were buttoned down the side. I've often wondered if other bikes like his were around at the time.

The year was roughly 1949 or 50 and I could see the steep hill looming up in front of me as I pedalled as fast I could. I was on my way back to the Office at the Albion Clay Co, where I worked, but mum had done stew for dinner and the dumplings were weighing heavy on my stomache.

I'd been trying for weeks to get dad to buy me a light weight bike, because the Raleigh I had was far too heavy for me and pushing it up that steep hill from Hartshorne to the Tollgate at Woodville, was too much of an effort. Dad knew how I felt, because he also had a Raleigh and he had to ride it to Rawdon Pit everyday, which was a round trip of roughly four mile - up hill all the way there and down hill most of the way back.

I pushed my feet hard down on the pedals to get a good run at the hill and hoped that I'd get past the bridge, but that was wishful thinking on top of mum's suet dumplings.

Suddenly, I spotted in my path ahead, what looked like a large coiled rope. 'Must have fallen off a lorry,' I thought and swerved to avoid it; but to my horror, the rope uncurled itself and got tangled up in the spokes of my bike wheel. I was thrown off and when I saw it was a snake, I dragged my cut and bruised body to the side of the road out of its way.

I didn't know one snake from another at that time, so it could have been an adder for all I knew. I sat there on the pavement and watched in amazement as it gradually freed itself and slithered off into someones garden. When I thought it was safe to move, I picked up my battered bike and pushed it all the way up the hill to the office.

After that, dad had no choice, he had to get me a new bike, so we went down to Swadlincote at the weekend and looked to see what the bike shop opposite Lushes had got, suitable for a girl of sixteen.

I saw the one for me in a corner of the shop. It was a Silver Flash racing bike with dropped handlebars. Very modern for the time period.

"You can't have that," said dad. "It's not for a girl."

"Course it is dad," I said. "It's got no crossbar," and after a lot of

EXCITING YEARS! • 79

1940's William Parry of Stone Row, Moira

persuasion he gave in. Neither of us had any idea of the importance that bike was going to play in my life.

I couldn't wait for Monday to come, just to see how fast I could go and how much more of that steep hill I could climb. Sure enough, I could get past the bridge, but I still walked the rest of the way up to the Tollgate, along with Jean Willis my office colleage and Peter Wallace who worked at Swad.

I was proud of my new bike and since the Managing Director, Mr Brookes, had assigned me to go up to the 'Big House' at Boothorpe, every day, to take letters etc., to Mr Lawton, I knew that my journey would be an easier one now that I had my Silver Flash. The road was only a cart track and not for the likes of the heavy Raleigh bikes.

I waved to the men unloading conduit pipes as I passed by, Everything was going fine, until I reached the narrowest part of the track, screened each side by a wall. I'd always had an uneasy feeling at that part of the journey; but this time the hair on the back of my head stood on end and with good reason; for standing astride his bike, in the middle of the track; blocking my way, was a large built young man with ginger hair, wearing round his face a khaki mask. I couldn't believe it, things like that didn't happen in the early 50's, crime was almost non existent, except for the odd poacher or so and here I was, facing goodness knows what.

I pulled up sharply, a few feet away from him and my mind went into overdrive.

"What do you want"? I said, trying to stop my voice from trembling.

"The money you've got in your saddlebag!" he replied, his voice somewhat muffled.

"I'm not carrying any money! I said, realising that he must have been watching me each day, to know what might have been in my saddlebag and then it dawned on me that there way no way he was going to let me go and if I'd been on the heavy Raleigh bike I'd 'ave stood no chance at all.

"I'm expected at the Big House!" I said, "and if I don't get there at the usual time, they'll come looking for me," but that didn't put him off, he just sat there, so, plucking up all the courage I had, which would fit on a threepenny bit, I began talking about anything and everything, while at the same time, slowly moving my handlebars until they were facing to my right; then terrified, I watched and waited for the moment to run. I knew I'd got to get it right first time,

For a brief second, his attention was diverted and he looked down at the floor, I spun my bike round and pedalled as fast as I could, back the way I'd come. I was thinking of the lorry I'd passed earlier. 'if only I could reach it,' I thought.

I turned the corner and there it was, within shouting distance. The man was hot on my heels. I could feel him breathing down my neck. I knew he was about to grab me, so I shouted "Help! Help!" as loud as I could.

The men on the lorry heard me and came running to my aid. The man behind me muttered something and I felt him ease off, but I daren't turn round until I felt it was safe to stop. When I did stop, I saw him heading off over the fields and he was soon out of sight.

For a month after that I had a police escort wherever I went. The policeman wore plainclothes and followed discreetly behind me. Even at the cinema he sat three seats behind. The well built man with ginger hair, wearing a khaki mask round his face was never found.

Walking in a mechanical and automatic fashion, I had passed this way many times before so I didn't have to watch for landmarks, my feet seemed to know the way. This left my mind free to wonder who had stolen my purse with so little in it, leaving me with no bus fare to get home. There was nothing else to do but walk.

I was tired and the journey home was four miles, but in the darkness it seemed longer and everything looked strange than in the daylight. Shapes were no longer buildings, hedges took on the role of monsters. Nothing was the same. I was trying hard not to feel frightened.

I tried to work out the best way to go. Up the steep hill which had street lights or the shorter way along the lane with no lights and no hill? I chose the lane. There were high hedges and footpaths and it would be quicker. My eyes were beginning to get accustomed to the darkness and I started on my journey. There were a few houses at first with mostly, unlighted windows.

I was sixteen and fit to run if need be. What had I to fear? It was a bold thought that lasted only a few more yards, for two round eyes blazed at me and I shrank back. Then the creature raced away. 'Probably a cat,' I thought, screwing up my courage once again.

Further on down the lane a small building loomed up out of the darkness. I felt sure it wasn't a house. As I came nearer I heard the most blood-thirsty wailing and screeching. It sounded like the devil in distress. I ran across to the other side of the lane and continued running until I suddenly remembered that it was Castle Cattery. That explained it all. I breathed with relief.

I hurried to the end of the lane and debated which way I should follow now. The road which was dimly-lit or the next dark lane? If I followed the road I would have to pass the White Lady Spring. I shivered. It was rumoured that a lady from the big house nearby had drowned herself in the reservoir many years ago. They said when it was foggy, or even slightly misty, she appeared in front of you when you were walking and beckoned you to go with her and you could never resist. Nobody knew where she was likely to take you or whether anyone had ever gone with her. I was too afraid to take the risk, especially as it was getting misty, so I hastily chose the dark lane, still referred to today as 'across Scott's'.

This lane was no more than a cinder path across a field. I had often walked that way on Sundays in summer, to take a bunch of flowers from Grandad's garden to the lady of the house. If there were no flowers, there was no work for Grandad the next week at the colliery.

From one bendy dark lane to another I would have to go, but it would be a shorter way home. Home! It sounded a wonderful word in my mind at that moment, but would I ever get there? I had to pause for a few moments to gather strength before I went up past the church.

Then I went wearily on again and as I neared the end of the lane, I thought I could hear footsteps, heavy but not fast ones. I stopped for a moment to listen, my heart in my mouth. Yes, unmistakably a man's footsteps. It was too dark to see, but I could hear them more distinctly now.

I began to hurry and so did the person following me. I refrained from running. If I had to do so later I would have more breath for it. When I reached the end of the cinder path, I could just make out the broken five-barred gate, well known to me from passing through it every Sunday.

If I put my best foot forward I would soon come to the church. I don't feel easy when I see gravestones at night, but common sense tells me that these silent witnesses cannot harm me. I often worship at this church, red brick, dark blue tiles, but now with the darkness enveloping them, my common sense seemed to have deserted me. The leaded windows showed up, shining and frightening. Anyone inside could see me, but I couldn't see them. On the other hand, I could say they couldn't get out, but I remained free.

As I walked along wearily, I had time to wonder who the man was following me for so long down the cinder path at this late hour. Would I be able to see his face if he caught up with me? My legs were so tired. I must have been walking for an hour. The lane spread a long way in front of me. The footsteps were getting louder and nearer. I kept going, praying as I went.

When I reached the manor house on the bend, I thought with trepidation of the story of old Doll Bath which people in the village recounted in whispers. She was said to be Lady Dorothy Bath of the manor house who was murdered by her lover. Her blood stained one of the slabs in the passage. They say she wanders at dark down the long drive, lined on both sides by bushes. Timid folk will not go near at night-time.

What was I do do? My legs refused to go any further without a rest. I had to stop. The brick wall of the boundary built in the 40's was never completed. It now formed the wide open drive. I had no choice. I slipped behind the big brick pillar and waited.

The man with the heavy footsteps was passing the pillar. I hardly dared breathe. He wasn't very tall and I couldn't see his face. It was a black mask to me.

When he had passed by the wall, I stayed where I was for a short time. All was silent. I crept out from my hiding place and took some deep breaths. Then, dusting the leaves from my coat, I set off on the last few hundred yards home, praying the man wouldn't have hidden somewhere and be waiting to accost me. I kept looking round warily all the way.

As I approached our cottage, I saw a light shining in a downstairs window. Surely, Gran wasn't up at this hour? Grandad was at work. I hoped I hadn't worried her. We had no phone even if I'd had the money to call her to set her mind at rest.

Cautiously I opened the door and made sure the heavy iron latch didn't squeak as it usually did.

At the far end of the room the scullery door was opening wider and wider. I took a deep breath and my hand went to my mouth in fear. Had the man who followed me got into our cottage ahead of me and lain in wait until I arrived? As I watched in terror a dark figure walked in carrying a...a..weapon.

It was GRANDAD with his trowel in his hand!

"And where have you been, my girl?" he shouted. "I followed you all the way across Scott's and past the church and then I lost you." He wasn't pleased.

I explained how I'd been followed by a man and how I'd hurried to escape him. Grandad had known I was in front and must have been trying to catch up with me.

"I was scared stiff and, just imagine, it was YOU all the time."

Now that my fear had gone I burst out laughing. I found it very funny. Grandad didn't see any joke. He didn't laugh. He never did. Strange really, I never, ever saw Grandad laugh.

Lloyds cycle shop in Swadlincote is a typical olde worlde type shop. Although it is small on the outside; inside it is like a treasure trove, for the shop is fully stocked with all kinds of accessories for the cycle, plus car accessories and small electrical goods for the home.

Mr and Mrs Hollins have been there from around 1982 and they have always sold Raleigh cycles, for which the older generation of Swadlincote are very familiar. A Raleigh took many a miner and pottery maker to work, but in their day the cycles were heavy, mostly black or dark green in colour and they were nearly all the same shape - Sit up and beg we used to call them, but they were always reliable and never seemed to wear out.

Now, in this Modern day and age, there are all kinds of cycles and shapes.

1999 Lloyds Cycle Shop, Left to Right: Brian Hollins, Mark Snea, Mrs Hollins, Paul Snea

There is the new micro bike, the folding bike and the ever popular mountain bike.

Today's world is a stressful one, no wonder it is geared toward making the most of our leisure time and the Raleigh cycles are still as popular and they are as good as they always were, but there is one outstanding feature, the frames of the 90's are made of aluminium, which makes them lighter in weight. Also, today's cycles can have as many as twenty seven speeds. The colours are much brighter too, maybe, that's because of today's world, the Motto is - Be bright - be seen at night. The emphasis has got to be on safe riding and don't forget your helmet, you will need one, they are an absolute must.

So, pack your sandwiches and get out there with your family in the countryside, but be prepared for all weathers, you know what british weather is like, you can get four seasons in one day and don't forget a map, just in case you get lost!

When I left School, I worked in the Accounts department at the Albion Clay Co. Ltd where the world of Upstairs/Downstairs was still in evidence. The head of the firm was known as 'Sir' and was looked on with great respect. A large painting of his father before him graced the walls of the office and caps were taken off before wishing his lady wife 'Goodmorning.' Servants looked after their forty roomed home.

We didn't have computers then; work in the Accounts department was done by hand. Every sale entry was made in a great thick heavy ledger of which we had four.

We had comptometers (electric adding machines) Cynthia Brearly and Barbara Clay ran those, but the man I worked with, Mr Arthur Smith, could add any column of figures faster than any comptometer. Sometimes, I used to stand behind him, watching him add the figures (which were in pounds shillings and pence) and often I tried to reach the answer before he did, hoping one day to equal the master.

We had to balanced all the books to the last penny, each month and sometimes, it took us a week to find it. But for job satisfaction, working in Accounts was the best.

I remember when you walked into Woolies, you walked through the right hand door, passed the pac a macs and the weighing machine and the first aisle had got biscuits; dozens of different sorts of biscuits, but it was the sweets that intrigued me. There was all sorts of sweets in the shape of cigarettes. They were all colours and there must have been about twenty different packets of sweet cigarettes you could get and in twenties. I'm an avid non smoker. I've never smoked in my life, but those sweet cigarettes have done my teeth more harm than ever real cigarettes could have done and I had another tooth out last week to prove it.

It seemed funny to see Woolworths tucked away between Mycrofts tobacconists and Wilton and Dythams Bazaar, on a photograph taken in 1938 of bygone days.

I couldn't remember it like that, but it just shows how ones memory can play tricks on the mind. It looked much better when it had a second storey put on top. It was more in keeping with the rest of the buildings.

The shelves all round the shop seemed to be in stages, the bottom shelves being very low down and just right for sticky fingers to reach out of a pushchair and remove a tasty looking sweet.

One day, I remember going to Woolworths with mum, when I was small. That morning, the handle had dropped off one of her cooking pans and dad's dinner, which was stew and dumplings, had gone all over the floor. He was non too pleased I can tell you and mum said. "Get yourself ready Joanne, we're going to Swad for a new pan and I quickly put me coat and hat on and we ran up the road to catch the bus. Mum had to drag me along, because she could walk quicker than I could.

We got on a Barton's bus - that was one of the posh ones; they had plush seats and it took us about 20 minutes to get to Swad.

"We haven't got long Joanne," she said. "We've got to get back before your dad goes to work. I've got his snap to put up for the Pit, so don't mess about in Woolies."

"Aw mum! I said. "There's such a lot of things to look at in Woolies. Can I have some sweets while we're there?"

"Only if you behave yourself," she replied.

Anyway, mum found a new saucepan and some sweets for me. She paid for them both at the counter and we went out of the shop; but as we were running for the bus, I pulled mum's sleeve.

"Mum! You forgot to buy the lid," I said.

"Shush Joanne!" she said. "No I didn't. We'll get the lid next week. I'll use the old one till then."

"But mum, it's got a big dent in it!"

"I know it has," said mum. "But I can't afford to buy the lid this week and you don't have to tell everybody with shouting Joanne. Come on the bus is coming."

And so, that was how it was at Woolworths, 50 odd years ago. Everything in the shop was either 3d (old money) or 6d (2 p) today's money. They sold electrical good, clothes, food and sweets and customers could buy things in stages eg: Saucepans 6d for the pan and 6d for the lid. Spectacle frames were 6d and lenses another 6d each. Things have certainly changed since then: but it's nice to know that Woolworths is still going strong.

Is it possible for an advert in the paper to change the direction of a person's life - it did for one man in the Polish Army. He was getting ready to set out and make a new life for himself and his wife and he began to look through the wanted adverts while he was stationed at Aylesbury. One advert he found of interest read - Lady Wragg of Swadlincote requires a gardener and a cook. Mr Baumgartner and his wife were prepared to take anything that came along, so they answered the advert, were accepted and came to live in Swadlincote.

Mr Baumgartner became a Butler and Mrs Baumgartner helped in the kitchen as a cook and they settled down to make their lives here. A year later, a son was born and they left the employment of Lady Wragg. Mr Baumgartner took a job at 'Greens' for a while, but he was a mechanical engineer and after taking a course on watch making, he set up his first shop in Alexander road, Swadlincote. With him at that time was a Mr Tribershephski and a young man name Mr Hillstone. 1952.

Time always brings change and many people remember the move to the shop in Market street, close to Richardson's Furniture store. Mr Hillstone joined him there, along with Peter Baumgartner. Horace Pickering and Rowena Taylor and the business became well established. The local people got used to the man who didn't speak with a South Derbyshire accent.

When the Pits began to close one by one and the time came for Swadlincote to put on its new image, the old Shambles as we called it, at the side of the Town Hall, was removed and four smart looking shops replaced it. Once again Mr Baumgartner and his staff: Peter Baumgartner. John Baumgartner. Mr Hillstone. Rowena and Ann Birket, moved, but this time it was into the third shop. His son Peter was involved in the business for a long time, but eventually, moved on.

EXCITING YEARS! • 89

1987 Left to Right: P. Baumgartner, Mr Baumgartner senior, Ann Birkett, Mr Hillstone, J. Baumgartner, Midland Road, Swadlincote. 3rd shop

Mr Baumgartner had been a familiar figure riding his cycle round town, but sadly, a few years ago he died after a fall from it and the business now carries on with his son John, whose mother is now 78 years old.

When Mr and Mrs Baumgartner first came over to Swadlincote, they must have found something of value here to make them stay, for Swadlincote had hardly begun to lose its chimnies, smoke and grime. We'd like to think it was the friendliness of the people of South Derbyshire. Anyway, whatever it was, they became part of the Swad we all knew and loved and like so many other dear familiar faces, Mr Baumgartner will not be forgotten and his business will continue we hope for many more years, through his son John and his faithful and friendly staff.

Long ago, when I had a waist and muscles, in what my daughter described as the 'Olden' days, at least that's what she always said when I tried to impart a bit of wisdom. "Dad, we are not living in the old days now." she'd say.

I was in the air force and amongst the junk we were issued with was a watch, a wind-up masterpiece, accurate and reliable.

It served me well through the war and afterwards, but stopped sometime in the 1950's. Being part of my person for so many years, I decided to have it looked at. In Alexandra Road was a small shop which undertook watch and clock repairs, called Baumgartners.

In I went with my service watch and said. "Can you look at this please?" He flipped open the back and said. "This is a very good watch," and then I told him about it being with me through the war. After looking inside, he said. "There's nothing broken, but it needs cleaning and oiling, come and collect it in two days."

Two days later, I went back to the shop. Mr Baumgartner said. "I cleaned it and put in a new glass for you as the other was badly scratched. I remember the bill was 12/6d, in real money. Remarkably, the watch still runs after fifty two years, but not every day. Rather a war memento than a daily timepiece. I must have a new strap put on it sometime.

One very cold day in January 1999, as a member of the South Derbyshire Writers Group, I had the privilege of interviewing the present members of the Dinnis family, at the shop in Swadlincote.

The shop has been there for many years and like Salt Bros, has represented stability in the town. I was pleased to see the High street full of people, despite the cold and the brightly lit shop was a welcome sight.

Looking at the various watches in the window, I remembered the first one I had was from Dinnis shop, when I was about six and I've no doubt that many of the local people of Swadlincote also bought their time pieces from Dinnis.

In those days the Miners in particular, were very proud of the silver watches and chains that hung on their waistcoats. But that was in a time when watches and clocks were works of art and much sought after today.

They were as beautiful inside as well as outside; mechanisms that worked on cogs and wheels that fascinated most children, when dads thought they were clever enough to mend their own watches after they'd dropped them, but always ended up with bits left over when they tried to put them back together again.

I went into the shop where it was warmer and when Mr Dinnis came in, his first thought was to ask for coffee for us and he took me towards a quiet room away from the busy sounds of the shop. He'd brought with him a number of Albums full of photographs of years gone by. The beginning of his family shop took us way back to the 1800's, when the trams were still running in Swadlincote. I was fascinated by the photographs representing those years.

Mr and Mrs Dinnis back then, John and Lavinia, had met in Exeter, while students together and they became teachers at the school in Church Gresley, known fondly as the 'GET WISDOM SCHOOL'. John was the organist at the Church and when they retired, a silver teaservice dated February 28th - 1885, was presented to Mrs L.Dinnis by the parishioners of Gresley as a token of their esteem.

In 1889, they opened the first Jewellers and Pawnbrokers shop in the High street Swadlincote, but it was at the bottom end (next to Needham's clothing shop) which is now closed. Outside the shop, on the wall, they had a clock, similar to the one outside Dinnis' today.

1988 Centenary of H. B. Dinnis & Son, Swadlincote. Congratulations to Mrs F. M. Dinnis from Swadlincote Chamber of Trade.
Also 21st Birthday of Simon John Dinnis

In the early 1900's, the shop and clock moved up to the middle of the High street, where it still is now and became Henry, son of John and lavinia. Opticians, watchmaker and Jewellers. Henry was born at Gresley and for many years was responsible for the maintenance of the Town Hall clock, which he wound up every week. He was also a member of Swadlincote Parish Church and at one period held office as sidesman. He was married to Gertrude and had two sons and two daughters. Henry died on June 1st 1948, aged 80.

Later, because there was no-one to carry on as Opticians, that was sold to Lancaster and Thorpe and the shop kept on as Jewellers and watch and clock repairers. The clock had to be replaced by another one, because it had eventually deteriorated.

The Dinnis family originally came from Littleham. They were Yeoman farmers.

The Mr Dinnis we have now at the shop, served his watch and clock apprenticeship and when he was 22, in 1971, he came into partnership with his father. (Mrs Dinnis, his mother is now 84).

1989, was a very special year in more ways than one. Not only was it the shop's centenary (100 years of trading) but Mr Dinnis' son, Simon, who had joined the business when he was 15, was now 21 and his father took him into partnership. The double celebration was held at the Stanhope Bretby.

Simon, is a qualified gemologist, FGA and also qualified in diamond grading DGA.

Just before I came away, I asked the lady who helped in the shop, Mrs Ball, how long she'd worked there, she replied "10 years, but Mrs Naylor before me, worked here 45years before retiring." I smiled at her, because I remembered something that was said to me years ago - People of South Derbyshire were well known for their loyalty and it's certainly true.

As I shook hands with Mr Dinnis, he added this remark, "We try to give as good a service as we can. That's probably why we've been able to continue as long as we have." I am sure that he is right. They have indeed given good service to the people of Swadlincote and I hope they will continue to do so for many more years.

One of our oldest shops in Swadlincote is Richardson's Furniture shop in Market Street, established 1874 and like some of the other businesses in town, they have kept up with the times; recognising the changing scene of household goods, they have endeavoured to supply the needs of today's modern world, while at the same time retaining their quality of service.

Although the outside of the building is not large, the interior is able to accommodate quality furniture and carpets on four levels.

Margaret Young has been in the trade 40 odd years. Peter and Barry Williams 31 years each and Garry Beardmore 30 years, so they have much of their experience to offer to the public.

Mr Richardson Boss has been there since 1947. He was born in Market Street, over the shop and as a child he played on the delph, remembering it as a lively bustling place and would dearly love to see it return to those exciting days. His words echo the thoughts of others.

The adjoining Pharmacy used to be run by Trissie nee Richardson and Tony Gardner but as with most businesses over the years, retirement brings change and it is now under the name of K Brennan.

The pharmacy is another example of recognising the needs of changing times. People living in the 90's are interested in alternative medicine and good health more than at any other time in the past and so the shelves are stocked with things to help people obtain a better quality of life.

On the photography side of the shop, the up to date equipment assures better photographs.

I started using a brownie camera when I was about nine, then moved on to a German box camera, which my uncle Norman had carried with him through the second world war. I never realised how important those early photographs would be, even though they were only in black and white and small in size. But when we write about the past, photographs can bring those early memories to life.

It was wonderful to use the new type cameras. No winding on. No gadgets to measure the light and no looking through the view finder at an object which appeared upside down. I always felt that they were for using while standing on your head. Anyway, the new type camera suits me fine. All I have to do is just point it at the object and press the button. However, I

When the market was on the delph there was a kiosk there and you could get Dythams icecream which was a local delicacy. I've never found anybody that didn't like Dythams icecream. Then when the market moved into believe it or not Market street, about 1960 - Dythams stall stood the market, but I remember it was from the back of a van.

did drop a bit of a clanger recently.

I tried to take a photo, but the button wouldn't press, so I took it back to the shop - "It won't work," I said.

"Could it be the batteries madam?"

"No," I said. "They're new."

"Are you sure there IS a film in the camera." said the assistant.

"Of course there's a film in the camera!" I replied. "I bought a new one only last week and my husband put the film in for me." The assistant turned the camera every which way, then decided to open it up. "I'm afraid there's no film in madam," she said, with a straight face. I stood there in total disbelief, because that had never happened to me before. "But there must be!" I stammered, trying not to laugh. "I gave it to him to put the film in."

She showed me the empty compartment where the film should be. "No wonder it won't work," I said, laughing and seeing that I could see the funny side, she laughed with me and as I walked out of the shop, I thought 'I bet that's given her something to talk about for the rest of the day.'

When I arrived home, the first thing I did was to look in the cupboard and there sat the new film still in its box.

"I got interrupted just when I was going to do it," said the hubby, "so I put it back in the cupboard, but then I forgot about it." I threw a newspaper at him. "Well," I said. "I've just had my most embarrassing moment because of that," and I decided not to trust him with it in future.

*Swadlincote's old library was a beautiful building.
It was situated almost at the top
of Alexander road, where the
Majestic Cinema used to be,
but the library was so
badly hit by subsidence
it caused a lot of problems.
It was in the old days,
when we had to be silent and
talk in whispers.
Mr Bill and Miss Caddy were there then,
and they used to have big trollies
with the books on,
and there was so much
subsidence,
that they daren't let go
the trollies,
because they would run away
from them. The floor
was running down hill.
It was such a shame
because, eventually,
the building had to
come down.*

Bill Jones, formerly of Linton, now living in Tavistock, Devon, started work in the ordinary way at Netherseal Colliery, as a lad and eventually, became manager of Boardman's Colliery, Hearthcote Road, Swadlincote and he remembers.

My Grandad, Teddy Barsby, was a bricklayer at Netherseal Colliery. A repairs team, including a new carpenter, got on top of the flat topped cage to go down the shaft to do some repairs. The rope of the carpenter's safety harness hooked over a steel rod in the shaft top gates.

As the cage went down, the carpenter went up until he was forced against the gate and the rope broke. He fell and landed on top of the cage and was grabbed by his mates. When he got back up, he went straight to the office and handed in his notice.

During the hard winter of 1947, I was maintenance fitter and together with Norman Ayre, we cleared the top of the cages during the night shift.

The ice had built up over the whole area of the cages in a rectangular block, eight feet high. There were icicles in the shaft sixty feet long, despite the fact that four huge brazier fires were burning continuously around the shaft top.

Netherseal closed in 1947 and there was a job at neighbouring pits for everyone who wanted one. The miners went to several local Collieries, but it meant that Linton and especially Linton Heath, was never again the tight knit community it used to be.

Ted Grice from Overseal, was about 18 when he worked at Gresley Pit and one day, the roof caved in. He was buried along with a Lay Preacher from Gresley and Ted has never forgotten the man.

The Preacher began to pray that rescue would come quickly, but in his prayer he was more concerned that young Ted would be rescued first, because he was young and had all his life before him, whereas he, the Preacher was a middle aged man and had seen much of life. The Preacher continued his prayer for Ted until finally rescue came.

They were both saved and Ted asked to be taken to his Grandma Millard's in second Pit Row and stayed there until he recovered from his injuries. Later, Ted went back down the Pit, but as an electrician.

The buildings of the old Shoddy Pit have now completely disappeared and the foundations of the old engine house were unearthed in 1944 approx; when pipes were being laid in John Street by Swadlincote UDC. The bridge Garage occupied part of the site and three shafts are under the raised lawn on the other side of John Street. These were provided with manholes.

The railway lines connected the Pit with the railway just beyond the station. These lines remained until the Burton and Ashby Light Railway ceased to run trams. The crossing at the foot of the bridge was always a headache for the Light Railway officials. The trams had to slow down to minimise the bump and then accelerate to get over the bridge, putting an almost impossible burden on the electric current. It was not until the trams ceased to run that it occurred to someone to cover up the 'crossing'

A relic of the old 'Shoddy' Pit is a clock in the possession of Mr H.B. Dinnis, of High Street Swadlincote. This used to hang in the Pit office and Mr Dinnis used it to check the time of other clocks and watches. It is still an accurate time-keeper.

It wasn't until 1959 that the headlines in the newspapers stated that the Miners had hit the £20 per week mark, £1,000 per year, which made them the best paid workers.

1900's The 'Old Shoddy' Swadlincote Pit

Going Going Gone

From 1947, as each Coal Pit closed, the men were gradually transferred to other Pits in the area, until finally, Donisthorpe, the last Pit, closed in 1990, leaving a kind of stillness in the air.

How many Miners, when their Pits closed, out of habit, rose early the next day, waiting for the sound of the hooters to blow as usual, but the day would only be met by the cry of the birds, greeting the morning and the wives, knowing the anguish of their husbands, would go about their work of cleaning the home in silence, broken only by a gentle pat on the shoulder now and then, with the words "Don't worry Bill, we'll manage, we always have."

The Pits nearest to Swadlincote, including its own, closed in the early 60's and the people living in the town itself soon began to notice a big difference in its appearance.

Gradually, the chimnies disappeared one by one. No more smoke or grime. The heavy dust laden air changed to an almost sweet freshness that the town had long forgotten. The washing on the lines gradually became clean and stayed clean, no longer flecked with brown blotches and spots. Shop windows lost their film of constant dust and metal dishes, pans and kettles, retained their brightness.

A great change indeed, but one for the better...

As the last Pit in the district closed, what was on the minds of those who were on that last shift and as they left the Pit bottom for the last time, surely there would be silence among the men in the cage as they slowly came up into the light; each man would be locked in his own thoughts.

Did they shake hands as men often do and say 'Cheers mate. All the best,' knowing full well that they might never see each other again, unless it was down at the local pub, or on the delph at Swadlincote and as they turned away, maybe a few did so with a tear in their eyes. After all, for some of them, it had been a lifetime, working down the Pit.

In some ways, their hearts must have been heavy, wondering what the

We used have a tea chest at the side of the fire. It'd got all our working clothes in and them moleskin breeches, they used be that wet sometimes they'd stand up on their own. How me mam used to put patches on I'll never know.

1998 Goodbye! The last shift. Rawdon

future was going to hold for them and their families. They had been used to that pay packet always being there at the end of the week, earned sometimes in blood and sweat. Would the redundancy pay out last long enough, or perhaps be invested rashly!

No-one likes change and for those not wanting to let go of the past, their wet moleskin trousers, heavy coats and belts would no doubt hang in the cupboard for a long time, before being cast away. Now, all that seemed left for them to do was to spend more time in the garden and no doubt some would welcome this. Others would take longer to adjust, living with a mixture of sadness for a while. But whatever way their new lives would take them, the people of Swadlincote will never forget the Miners and the fact that they lived with danger every day of their lives.

LIST OF COALMINES IN THE AREA

NETHERSEAL	1955 - 1947
RESERVOIR	1851 - 1948
BRETBY	1872 - 1962
SWADLINCOTE	1852 - 1965
GRESLEY	1812 - 1967
GRANVILLE	1823 - 1967
MEASHAM	1850 - 1986
CADLEY	1860 - 1988
RAWDON	1821 - 1989
DONISTHORPE	1871 - 1990

DARBYSHIRE BORN N BRED

I wer Darbyshire born n bred.
An' you know wot folk say about that.
You'n got plenty a brawn in ya bonny arms,
But you'n got nowt under ya 'at.
Folk could be rate an' all.
Cos I tried to talk posh, you say.
But when I met up wee 'em at th' shops,
All they did wer lof an' mek fun of may.
"It's cos you'n not got it rate," said Molly me friend.
"Be thee sen, an' thill all com round."
So I started to talk broad Darbyshire agen,
An she wer rate, cos that's just wot I found.
Well, I wer only tryin' to better mesen.
Or, so that's wot I thought ath time.
But it wer daft changin' wot I'n known all me life.
Broad Darbyshire suits may jus' fine.
An' I'll tell ya this. You'll find no better folk.
They're honest an' loyal an' true.
An' I'm proud to be Darbyshire born n bred.
An' I'm gooin' stay Darbyshire through an' through.

SOUTH DERBYSHIRE DIALECT.

The South Derbyshire dialect increased in the 19th and 20th century, with the industrial community, but since the closure of the coal, clay and pot industries, the dialect is gradually on its way out. At least we can save some of it by recording it for posterity. Below are some of the more familiar and not so familiar sayings. Read it as it is written and all will become clear.

ANNOYANCE AND FRUSTRATION.
Flippin' eck.
Arl goo tath foot of ar stairs.
Fryin' anover and flippin arry.
Floppin Jimmy Westcott.

EXPRESSIONS USED FOR PEOPLE WHO WERE NOT VERY BRIGHT.
Soft as a biled turnip.
Aze a proper gawby.
Aze gorra tile loose.
Aze lost somer 'is marbles.
Ay wuz on back row when breens wa gen out.

IF ANYBODY WAS LATE FOR WORK.
Ar neely didna com at all, cos ar wuz buzzed.

SOMEONE GOING TO CHURCH REGULAR, BUT VERY WAYWARD FOR THE REST OF THE TIME.
E'rs a Sunday Saint and a wick dee divil.

IF WE ASKED SOMEONE WHERE THEY HAD BEEN AND THEY DIDN'T WANT TO TELL, THIS IS WHAT THEY WOULD SAY.
Theer an back to say ow far it is.

A FOOTBALL MATCH WHEN THE CENTRE FORWARD HAS MISSED AN OPEN GOAL, SOMEONE WOULD SHOUT.
Ay cudna it a ball in a tray.

Going down the street, I saw a man being followed by his dog, about 10 yards behind. The man turned round and saw his dog following him, so he pointed his finger at it and said. "Wom it." The dog must have understood South Derbyshire, for it tucked its tail between its legs and went off wom (home)

WHEN WE SEE BLACK CLOUDS GATHERING WE'D SAY.
Bar gum, its black oer Bill's mother's.

WHEN SOMEONE HAD A NASTY EXPERIENCE.
Ar wa frit death.

LOOKING FOR SOMEONE.
'Av bin all over th' ockey lukkin fa yo.
Ya canna say fa lukkin.

PAIN IN THE HEAD AND KNEE.
Doctor - Ar kape gettin' this peen in me yed.
Arn gorra neel in me nay.

Pits and pots and pipes and muck
and the usual greeting of 'Aye up me duck'
This was South Derbyshire yesterday
pits all gone now, good riddance some say.
Who wants to work down a deep dirty hole
on hands and knees like some muscle bound mole.

But it wasn't all digging and breaking their back
or bringing home noggins of wood in their pack.
Each pit was a family the kinship was right
for work in the darkness or play in the light.
That strength and that pride along with the trust
passed on to accept change when they must.

But walk any street now clear of the muck
still hear the greeting of 'Aye up me duck'

chapter three
Life after Salts

All Change

*No pits. Some pots and pipes that's true
crockery stripes, some valuable too.
Cream mixing bowl never losing it's style
clean out the mixture, remember and smile.
Pots of no use, but for beautiful gifts
made by hard work and long weary shifts.*

*Our bathrooms and pipes led the world at one time
each factory spewing it's own smoke and grime.
Most of it gone now, what's left must work clean
soon where the slag heap, the spoil tips have been.
Trees of all shapes so as years come and go
they'll hide the hard surface, but inside we'll know.*

*What it was like for the people now gone
'Lest we forget.' Please pass it on.*

I think the people of my generation were the people who saw the biggest changes, possibly ever. When you think that before the war, down in London they had TV with a radius of about 10 miles, if you were lucky. Very few people before the war had a car. My father had one. Then all of a sudden, the war came and we had aeroplanes chugging along at 90 mile an hour. But after the war, we got things flashing around the skies. You could fly to Canada in what - 8 hours and I mean, at one day, you had to go by ship. We've seen all the inventions. TV, Computers, Videos, Gas fires; you name it we've seen it. So much has happened in basically such a short time. I believe it was possibly due to the war. I suppose that really pushed things along.

Have you ever noticed, you never see a policeman these days. But if you went back in time to 1983, you would.

The first thing you would notice was a lot less traffic and it was at that time, that the Derbyshire Constabulary introduced six residential police officers pounding the beat in the Swadlincote area.

The scheme started off with four officers based in Swadlincote. It was successful, so it was extended to six officers; three on foot and another three on bicycles.

The area they covered, was Castle Gresley, Linton, Overseal, Coton in the Elms, Rosliston, Cauldwell and Coton Park.

To meet the public, a policeman would certainly have to do a great deal of pedalling, covering fifteen to twenty miles a day, on one of the sturdy bikes of that time - the Raleigh.

The job of the policemen on bikes, was to reassure people and to be available. It was a matter of the public telling them what was happening so that they could sort things out.

Figures released by Derbyshire Police at that time, revealed that community policing was indeed sorting things out in the Derby East area, where the scheme had been tested. There was a twenty six per cent drop in burglary and a decrease in other serious crimes.

But time has moved on and the busy roads of today would not be suitable for the sturdy sit up Raleigh and the howling sirens of the police cars alert us to the fact that crime in all areas still goes on.

When the dark nights came round, the streets were lit by gas lamps in Newhall, and it became the centre for us boys to gather for an hour or so. Joe Lock the lamplighter came round each night with his pole, to switch the lamps on, and about 10-O-Clock he repeated the journey to turn the lights out. He did this every night irrespective of the weather.

SCALE DEVISED BY ADMIRAL SIR F. BEAUFORT 1774-1857

I referred to this scale and found that strong gales blow from numbers 9,10,11,12, - 12 being above 75 m.p.h. This describes the freak wind of the 1970's, which we very rarely get in this country thank goodness. It moved down this island at terrific speed in a large horseshoe shape.

On its way, it removed roofs from houses with ease and the final count was approximately 19,000,000 trees blown over and forests wrecked.

My own loss was less. In fact, I lost one tree and one greenhouse. The greenhouse frame was tied into knots and the covering was never found. The tree was a very large hawthorn, the trunk being one and a half feet thick and when I looked down the field in the morning, it was lying down with a huge hole where the roots had been torn out of the ground. As I looked at the damaged tree, I thought what a sight it was in the Springtime, covered with white blossom, which in the lightest breeze would shed like snow across the field. Never again would this occur, for the tree was dead. It was eighty years old and was stricken in one savage hour.

I went down the field with the chainsaw a week later and as I was reducing it to logs, I noticed that there was a magpie's nest at the top of the tree, consisting of sticks and milk bottle tops, but NO DIAMOND RINGS... The hedgehogs that had reared young, under the roots for years, would be looking for a new nesting site. Knowing nature as I do, they are very adaptable, except when crossing the road, so they will have moved to new roots and produced many more generations of hedgehogs.

When the new supertype stores began to emerge in the High street, they were so different from anything we'd ever known.

We were used to going into a shop, being served by a counter assistant, who weighed whatever we needed, wrapped it up, adding up the cost in his or her head (or on a scrap of paper) took the money and gave us the change. But to go into one of these new type shops for the first time was frightening, because the method of shopping there was against everything we'd been taught.

To begin with, there was all these shelves stacked with tins of food, cereals and fruit; everything in fact that we could possibly need, but we had to have a basket or a trolly and fill them ourselves, before taking them to the checkout! There was even cat and dog food. Our pets had all been used to having the same food as we ate, except for the odd bone from the butcher. But now they had a much larger choice.

Walking round the shop with a trolley full of goods that we hadn't yet paid for, felt very wrong and left us with guilt feelings to cope with, this of course was from our upbringing. It took weeks and weeks before we older ones got used to shopping this way. I then had another problem to handle.

I used to take my mother shopping with me, but she never did get to understand that everything had to go into a trolley first, before it was paid for; she kept putting everything into the shopping bag we had.

It took me so long to sort things out at the checkout, I was always very conscious that the person behind me in the queue probably had a bus to catch, so I couldn't wait to get outside fast enough - my nerves shot to pieces.

It got such a nightmare, I eventually, had to leave mum at home. When I finally did get the hang of it, I began to enjoy it. The only thing about it then was the fact that I usually spent more than I'd planned to spend, but then doesn't everybody do that.

There's no doubt that if Salts had stayed on they would have had to adapt their shops to this method, to keep up with the times. I wonder if they saw it coming!

We never gave it a thought did we that one day we wouldn't be using our usual £-s-d (pounds, shillings and pence) It had taken us a lifetime to learn it all and we were quite happy thank you very much, with our old coins and the use of the odd guinea or two on special occasions.

We also had Rods, Poles and Perches and so many ounces to the pound for making puddings and cakes and cwts, that's (hundred weights) to calculate the coal; but all of a sudden, it all changed. Do you remember 1971? Decimal Day they called it, when we no longer had our familiar monetary system. We had to learn a new one.

Just when the old grey cells were beginning to forget a few things like:

In them days they used have the birch you know. I remember 6 lads breaking into the shop in Alexander Road, when I went to Hastings Road school. All they took was toffees and pop - no money, no cigarettes, no chocolate, just pop and sweets. They got six strokes of the birch rod each. They never did nothing after that.

Where did I put me keys and have I put the cat out and locked the door and did I switch the cooker off. I'd better go back and check. You see what I mean! I'm the one that has to do all the checking when me and Ethel go to the shops. It seemed daft to us at our time of life having to start all over again and learn another way of adding up. It was like going back to school.

Now, we no longer get a dozen roses in a bunch, we only get ten. How can you be romantic and buy the wife roses cos you stayed out too late the night before, when they only give you ten. It's not the same is it and with Ethel and me on the pension, I can't afford two bunches.

Ethel's always complaining about her new tape measure. It's got centimetres on one side and inches on the other and when she's making something, she sometimes turns it over on the wrong side by mistake and cuts it too short. Last week, she chucked the tape at me." I'll use me old un," she said. "I'm fed up with this new one, I can't work out these centimetre things. Get me some sellotape Bill and I'll patch me old un up. It'll see me out."

Now, with these decimal coins, there's only a hundred pennies in a £ (pound) not the two hundred and forty pennies, like it used to be. I ask you, what can you make of that. I can't work it out for the life of me. Someone's on the losing end you know and I bet it's not them others.

Me and Ethel have still got drawers full of the old coins. Pennies, hapennies, farthings, threpanny bits and a few sixpences, but Ethel's have all got holes in, where I once made em into a bracelet for her.

We haven't got any guineas mind you, never did have any of them and we spent all the halfcrowns we'd got, which was all of three. Still, they all might become valuable one day if we keep em long enough; but I'm not so sure about that, cos we're both over eighty now. Still it's not worth bothering about, is it!

For as far back as I can remember, there has never been a swimming pool in Swadlincote. I was introduced to the pleasures of swimming in Matlock Lido, when I was at the Amber Valley Summer camp.

When I came back from there, I still wanted to carry on swimming, but the schools in the 40's didn't have their own swimming pools, as many of the modern schools have today. Everybody had to travel on the bus to the nearest swimming baths, which for me was situated at the end of Burton bridge - the old bridge - not the new one. St Peters, at Stapenhill wasn't built then.

At Burton there were two pools, both indoors. The larger pool was deep at one end with three diving boards. The other was for learners. It was always crowded. We had to either climb the iron frame spiral staircase to reach the cubicles for changing, or go up the concrete steps at the other end of the baths, but they were so cold. I always went for the spiral staircase. I was used to that, because at home we had a wooden spiral staircase to the bedrooms.

Swimming suits for ladies were often home knitted and were very heavy when in water. All the families wore a cap then, to protect the hair from drying out too much, but swimming caps left much to be desired; they felt very rubbery and fit so close to the head, that when they were taken off, the hair was just lank, flat and had lost any bounce it may have had in the first place.

It took such a long time to get there on the bus, I didn't go very often, but I always used to think - 'Wouldn't it be nice if Swad had a pool,' and then something magical happened.

With the gradual closure of some of the pits, pots and pipe works; Swadlincote began to change its old image and put on a new one. One of the first changes to come was a Leisure Centre, now known as Green Bank and it has just about everything you could want, including a large pool and a smaller one for children. It was wonderful.

The difference in today's swimming caps is very obvious, not many people wear one at all. But when I first went to the pool, I managed to get a cap with flowers all over it. That was great and I wore it with pride, along with the modern swimming suits. My hat gave the children a laugh, but I didn't mind that and this time, I was able to go every week and began to build up my stamina.

If Swadlincote had never had any other improvements, I've certainly been very grateful for the pool and I bet I'm not the only one.

My husband tells the story of when he was a little boy at Coton Park, in the 30's. On Saturday mornings, some ten young lads from Coton Park used to set off, with a bottle of water and some sandwiches. The lads as he can remember, were the Johnny Bradley brothers, Wilf Bradley, Ron Miller, Tom Ramsel Elywn Meakin, Vic Yates and others.

They played a game tossing a coin to walk or run across a field. Twenty one in all from Coton Park, to Stapenhill, then over the Iron Bridge 'Ferry' to be precise.

It took about an hour in all to reach the swimming pool. Sometimes, as they ran through the fields, they were chased by cows and fell on cowpats. Other times they had saved enough to buy some windfall apples from a friendly farmer. At the Burton Baths, they played a game of diving for things that would sink to the bottom of the pool, old washers, or pennies.

My parents, Frank and Ivy Liversuch, lived for a while in the flat attached to the baths. Like the baths it was gloomy and at times they felt the place was haunted. Certainly, their dog, a large Alsation, would sometimes stand still as though in fear, the hairs of his body sticking up.

To go round the baths late at night, with my dad, (who was the caretaker) whilst he locked up, was an eerie experience. You would be in one of the rooms and suddenly hear doors banging in another, but there would be no one there. My mother was standing at the kitchen sink one day and felt someone touch her on the shoulder, she turned round thinking it was her husband, but there was no one there.

My youngest sister always felt uneasy at night and the dog would sleep outside the bedroom door, sometimes, it would scratch to come to her and was obviously frightened. My dad said he once thought someone had committed suicide there, I don't know.

On the lighter side, when the Circus came to Burton, they would set up in the meadow against the baths. In the morning, the elephants would be brought up to an outside tap at the flat and there, they would be watered and spray water with their trunks at each other.

I remember going through iron gates and a heavy door, paying a halfpenny entrance fee. There was a lot of Victorian tiles from the changing rooms to the pool and you had to go through a disinfectant trough. There was also a long pole with a net at the end, in case anyone was in danger of drowning.

I remember having a rope tied round me to teach us to swim. We had to wear bathing caps then and our feet were inspected. There were no bikinis either and if you forgot your towel, you had to pay to borrow one and give it back as you went out.

I found it a depressing building, so different from the baths at Swad, where I go with other Senior Citizens.

After the second world war, when building materials were available, new buildings gradually appeared in the town of Swadlincote and its new image was well under way by the late 70's. Then a questionnaire was sent to the people, asking them which project they would like to see come to completion. Many were in favour of a swimming pool and the history of the Leisure Centre begins here.

On March 22nd 1978, the first phase of the South Derbyshire Leisure Centre was opened by Jack Charlton, who was accompanied by his wife and son.

Three years later, Swadlincote had a visit from the Princess Royal, to officially open the new multi purpose Sports Hall at the Leisure Centre.

LIFE AFTER SALTS • 115

1978 Jack Charlton, Swadlincote Leisure Centre

A Right Royal Welcome

When Princess Anne visited Swadlincote in Oct. 1981, she arrived by helicopter at the Pingle School playing field. Waiting to greet her there were crowds of local children, ready to give her a warm Swadlincote welcome.

The Princess wore a deep blue coat, with a blue and turquoise hat, navy handbag, gloves and shoes to match. She was greeted by Colonel Peter Hilton, the Lord Lieutenant of Derbyshire and local dignitaries. Then she met some of the children.

One of the first youngsters to meet the Princess was Simon Tunnicliffe. She then spoke to a group of boys from Pingle School, Jamie Ross, Simon Britnall and Daren Dicken. At the Pingle School, the Princess was welcomed by Michelle Derry, Loraine Book and Rachel Locker. She then made her way back to the South Derbyshire Leisure Centre, where she was introduced to South Derbyshire District Council vice-chairman, Councillor Brian Valentine and his wife Janice.

After more introductions, the Princess went into the Swimming pool area and met members of East Staffs Handicapped and Youth Sports and Social Club who were swimming in her honour.

In the Main Hall, Princess Anne presented the Duke of Edinburgh Awards to over 60 children and afterwards Joy Peat presented the Princess with a large basket of flowers on behalf of the Brownie pack. Joy's five year old brother also presented the Princess with two stuffed toys for her children.

This was followed by the Royal walkabout which took in Market Street, the Delph and West Street. Represented in the route was the Army Training Corps, Gresley Scouts, Brownies and the Women's Royal Voluntary Service, also a group of fifteen from the Swadlincote Task Force.

Andrew Harris, a two year old, presented the Princess with a posy of dahlias from his mother's garden. His grandmother, Mrs Molly James, had brought him to see Princess Anne.

The South Derbyshire Youth Band played during the walkabout in which the British Red Cross, St. Johns Ambulance Brigade and the Chamber of Trade were represented.

LIFE AFTER SALTS • 117

1981 Princess Anne meets Women's Royal Voluntary Service members, the Delph, Swadlincote

Princess Anne

At the commemorative gardens at the Grove site, the Princess was handed a pair of golden scissors on a cushion, by Councillor Roy Nutt and she cut a blue ribbon above the plaque to commemorate the wedding of Prince Charles and Lady Diana.

In the Grove hall, she unveiled a plaque, officially opening the all purpose Sports Hall and took tea with Civic Dignitaries, receiving a gift of oven to tableware - TG Green & Co Ltd, from the South Derbyshire District Council Chairman, Councillor Nutt.

There were more cheers for the princess later, as she arrived back at the School for her departure at 5.15pm. She walked to the edge of the field and gave a final wave as she boarded the waiting helicopter.

It had been a wonderful day for the people of Swadlincote to remember and especially all the children who received the Duke of Edinburgh Award for their achievements.

There's a lot of work goes into a Royal visit; everyone wanting their part to run smoothly and especially since Swadlincote hadn't had a Royal visit for over 50 years, when the Duke of Kent inspected a centre for the unemployed at Park Road, Church Gresley. So, on the day of Princess Anne's visit in 1981, everything seemed to run smoothly and all the crowds were left with fine memories to cherish, but I wonder, how many of those who were there knew anything about the drama that was taking place in the High Street. Let's see what happened...

Just before Salts closed all its shops in Swadlincote, in 1982, I was involved in an incident that I shall never forget. It happened on the day of a Royal visit to the town.

There were crowds of people on the delph in Swad, waiting to see the Royal visitor and although they must have heard the alarms going off, they were not aware that it was at one of the Salts shops in the High Street and there was quite a drama taking place.

It was lunch time and one of the customers wanted some towels or something and Salts were well known for going out of their way to help the customer get what they wanted.

I'd moved from the haberdashery department, to the hardware

When you had your anniversary, you used have a new frock, and you'd go and get it from Salts.
But the first weekend it closed down, in 1982, I got on the Trent bus and went down the following week for something for me husband.

He asked me to bring him something from the hardware department.
I got off the bus at the bottom of Hill Street, and just stood there, and couldn't think where to go for it, because, you just automatically went to Salts for whatever you wanted.

LIFE AFTER SALTS • 119

1982 Left to right back row: C. Mathews, Sharron C. Storer, F. Peck, S. Price, R. Parker, Wendy ?, Mr Henry, C. Eames
Left to right front row: P. Glover, Mrs Smith, Maureen ?, Mrs Meakin, Mrs Young. Salts Staff

department, which was opposite Woolworths, but I felt sure that I'd seen what the customer required at the haberdashery store, which was further up the High Street, so I went to get them for her.

As I reached the top of the stairs in haberdashey, they had these light sensor things and I didn't even know that there was an alarm system.

Suddenly, there were bells and sirens going everywhere. It was so loud, you couldn't hear yourself think and everybody outside was wondering what was going on.

I ran back to the hardware department and tried to find one of the managers, but they'd all gone for dinner. Someone said there should be a key somewhere to switch the alarm off and one of the girls said she knew what the key looked like, so, she tried to find it amongst a bunch of keys that one of the staff produced, but she said. "It's not there, someone's taken it off the key ring."

The only thing left to do was to ring one of the Mr Salts, son. He lived at Westfield Drive and he came down to switch the alarm off and said he could hear it going from where he lived.

It was all panic stations really, because of the Royal visit. Princess Anne was due to arrive shortly, by helicopter. There were police milling about everywhere. Anyway, the alarm was finally switched off just in time and the visit went without a hitch, but it did cross my mind that I might lose my job. However, I didn't. After all, I was only trying to help a customer in the first place.

I used to clean the windows when I was a young lad, at Salts shop and because I was tall, I could reach the top of the windows. One of the Mr Salts used to come out and say. "Have you nearly finished John (although me name was Arthur) that didn't matter. I think they called everybody John there, I suppose it was with the amount of staff we'd got. Anyhow, if I'd missed a bit, he'd say. "Do them all again John!"

In 1979, the South Derbyshire District Council's Recreation and Amenities Committee, began the entertainment programme at the new multi purpose hall at the Leisure Centre, with a concert by the Webb Ivory Newhall Band and the Gresley male voice choir, followed by Grimethorpe Colliery band. An evening of folk music and the East Midland Dance Co.

Remember these:-

SNOOKER - An exhibition snooker match featuring Ray Reardon and Willie Thorne 1979.
Tony Knowles and Jimmy White, staged by Newhall
Nationally famous snooker referee, Len Ganley 1981.

WRESTLING - Featuring Jackie (Mr TV Pallo) The Canada Concert. South Derbyshire's Youth Band and choir. 1979.

DARTS - Eric Bristow and Maureen Flowers exhibition match 1980.

PANTO - Cinderella 1982
Jack and the Beanstalk Grove Hall 1983
Mother Goose 1985

These are just some of the many events that have taken place over the years, at the Leisure Centre and Grove Hall, since they were first opened.

Did you know that early in 1982, Swadlincote had its very own Swad Ness Monster, called 'Swaddie.' Mark Chadbourne first saw the monster lurking in the depths of the pool at the Leisure Centre at Swadlincote and he reported it in the Burton Mail.

Swaddie had come to show the children what fun they could have in the pool, instead of sitting at home watching too much television on Saturdays and this was no man eating monster, Swaddie was a great big inflatable softie, 15 feet long, with a head and fins and it loved to float about the pool seeing how many children it could carry on its back. By the looks on the faces of 18 children, they all thought that Swaddie was great fun, but what I'd like to know is - has Swaddie been seen since! Perhaps, he has moved

1980's Swadness Monster meets children at Swadlincote Leisure Centre

on to another patch, but if he ever comes back, he'd better watch out, because there's an inflatable new Robo Ant, floating about the pool at Swadlincote Leisure centre and he's no softie.

On November 18th 1988, it was Fund raising day for the Children in Need, but this day was different to all the others they'd had. It was to be an exciting day, because the whole town of Swadlincote including the villages beyond, really excelled themselves, by helping to raise thousands of pounds and they had the privilege of being one of the Host Towns involved. It put Swadlincote on the map, because they were able to see their efforts televised.

Maybe you were part of the activities of that day.

The fund began in 1927 and when the appeal was launched on radio, it raised £1,143 and continued every year on radio until 1979. In those fifty two years £630.898 was collected.

Since the appeal was televised in 1980, the amount raised has gone up beyond all expectations. A BBC spokesman said, This year, donations could bring the overall sum donated in the appeal's sixty four year history, to over £100 million and in fact the hosts of Children in Need at that time, Terry Wogan and Sue Cook, later said thank you to all viewers who helped to make 1991 so successful. The fund is still being run in 1998 and the donations keep rising every year.

*When Princess Diana came to visit
Swadlincote in 1991,
Louisa Jane Bennett, a fair haired
little girl of seven,
was chosen to present her with a
bouquet of flowers.
It was a day that
Louisa will never forget.
Her friends at Pingle School,
all thought that it was
wonderful to be able to
meet a real princess and
especially one who was loved
by so many people.*

*When the great day arrived,
Princess Diana smiled at her,
and the first thing she said to Louisa,
was "What a pretty dress."
Louisa smiled back at the Princess and
offered her the flowers and said.
"Hello. Here's a bouquet of flowers,
from all the people in Swadlincote,
and the Princess replied
that she was happy to receive them.*

*It certainly was an exciting moment
for all those present.*

January 16th 1991 was a very special day for the people of Swadlincote. Princess Diana, the Princess they all loved, was paying Swadlincote a visit.

The crowds waiting on the delph in the freezing cold, muffled up with coats and scarves were there, just to catch a glimpse of the Princess. But first, they had to wait a while, for her first stop was at Church Gresley, the pottery makers Cloverleaf TG Green, was celebrating their bi centenary.

The Princess was greeted by the Lord Lieutenant of Derbyshire, Colonel Peter Hilton and his wife, Mrs Winifred Hilton. Princess Diana was wearing a three quarter length Cerise jacket with a blouse buttoned to the neck, black pleated skirt, shoes and gloves to match.

She then greeted Council officials and members of the company. These were Councillor Josiah Ford, chairman of South Derbyshire Council and Mrs Hetty Ford: Mr Terry Day, council chief executive, Mrs Pat Day, Mr Richard Smith, Cloverleaf TG Green managing director: Mr Graham Lowe, financial director: Mr Jeremy Redshaw, senior production manager: Mr Frank Molnar, production manager and Mr Andy Smith, operations director. Miss Sharon Martin, a laboratory assistant, age 17, from Church Gresley, presented the Princess with a posy.

Inside the factory, Princess Diana spent several minutes talking to Mr Gerald Talbot, age 48, from Newhall, whose job includes putting handles on jugs and teapots. He has been with the company 22 years.

The Princess told George Smith age 54, a turner for 37 years, that he ought to be on The Generation Game.

Mrs Susan Foster was asked if working at the factory was a family tradition and Susan replied that it was, since her mother had worked there before her.

The Princess also spoke to Mrs Alison Goodwin from Midway, who applied transfers to pottery products, following which Princess Diana removed her gloves to lend a hand.

Outside, the crowd were eagerly waiting for the Princess to emerge from the building and later, she moved on to open the company's new bottle kiln museum.

One of the next calls on her busy itinerary was to open Church Gresley Indoor Bowling centre, where she met Mr Ken Toon, chairman of the centre.

He gave the Princess a miner's safety lamp and told her the lamp had saved many miner's lives.

The Princess was then invited to bowl a wood. She took her shoes off and enjoyed a game with President Mr Ray Smith.

Ever willing to show her caring attitude, her next stop was Granville Court Sheltered Housing scheme in Swadlincote. She was first greeted by a group of children from Belmont Primary school and members of Newhall Rainbows. The children had been given a few hours off school to see the Princess.

Darryl Whyatt aged 10, from Springfield road school, thought she was very pretty and other remarks from the youngsters were, "Now that's what I call a Princess!" and rightly so.

The Princess chatted with residents from Oaklands Aged People's home. "I couldn't take my eyes off her, she was so beautiful," said Mrs Florence Parker. "I never thought I'd ever shake hands with Royalty," said Phyllis Latimer.

South Derbyshire's Councillor, Mrs Betty Oakey then escorted the Princess inside Granville Court and gave her a guided tour of the accommodation, before stopping to chat to Mrs Olive Fairbrother of Drayton Street, Swadlincote, in the dining room, where residents and specially invited guests had gathered for lunch. Mrs Fairbrother chatted with the Princes on developments in the Middle East.

It was then time for the Princess to help three of the luncheon guests to mark their birthdays. First she met Mrs Elizabeth Morris, who was 101, on Boxing day. Followed by Mr Ronald Collie who was 90 and Mrs Emily Salt, who was also celebrating her birthday.

After cutting a very special birthday cake with Mr Collie, the Princess joined Mrs Margaret Johnson of Chestnut Avenue Midway, at the piano.

Princess Diana unveiled a plaque to commemorate her visit, she then took a short well needed rest. Later, she signed a glorious portrait of herself for the residents of Granville Court to enjoy.

Next stop, the delph and as always Princess Diana was happy to meet the people. Sally Tivey of Winshill had waited two hours with her small son Benjamin in the extreme cold to see the Princess; but it was worth waiting for, she said.

The Princess gradually made her way to Grove Hall and before going inside,

LIFE AFTER SALTS • 127

1991 Visit of Princess Diana on the Delph, Swadlincote

1991 Left to right: Mrs Bennett, Louisa Bennett, Edwina Currie, Princess Diana, Josiah Ford

128 • INTO THE LIGHT 2000

1991 Time off from school to greet a royal visitor, Princess Diana

1991 Face in the crowd with a big welcome

she was greeted by Councillor Wilf Heap, chairman of South Derbyshire Recreation Amenities Committee and Mr Ian Reid, director of technical Services.

Princess Diana was cheered as she planted a five year old English Oak in the Hall grounds, before going inside to meet local business civic dignitaries, South Derbyshire MP Mrs Edwina Currie and representatives from other organisations in the district.

Diana, a tireless worker for charities, was pleased to know that Burton Mail readers also showed great interest in helping local charities. She told charity worker Mr Bernard Le Blond she was interested in the Heatbeat Appeal and the Burton Scanner Appeal.

As she left the Hall, a guard of honour was formed by the 1211 Swadlincote Squadron of the ATC, then she walked towards her waiting Jaguar, but paused to accept more flowers from Lisa Wileman, aged eight.

Princess Diana had really enjoyed the friendliness and hospitality of the Swadlincote people and just before she got into her car and was whisked away, she smiled and said.

"I'll be back."

Comments

On such a memorable day for Swadlincote, the friendliness of its people had shone through and I am sure that had it been possible; Princess Diana would have kept that promise to return. However, despite the extreme cold, she left behind an unforgettable day filled with joy and laughter, a day regarded by the people of Swadlincote, as a great honour and privilege to have had such a distinguished and much loved visitor as Princess Diana and it was one they will never forget.

August 31st 1997, turned out to be a day like no other. The knowledge that Princess Diana had died in a car crash in Paris, plunged the whole nation into disbelief and gloom.

She died alongside Dodi Fayed and the driver, Henri Paul, in the Mercedes they were travelling in. The bodyguard, Trevor Rees Jones was the only survivor.

The following days were filled with sadness and the mountain of flowers placed outside the gates of Kensington Palace continued to grow, until it became a mass of colour. The nation poured out its grief, no one tried to hide their tears. The cards with the flowers showed just how heartfelt that grief was; the words lay unspoken but there for all to see.

Diana s funeral took place on Saturday, September 6th 1997, in Westminster Abbey. Her coffin, mounted on a gun carriage, slowly made its way from the Royal Chapel to Westminster Abbey. The streets were lined with people and behind the gun carriage, walking in silence, was Prince Phillip, Prince William, Earl Spencer, Prince Harry and Prince Charles.

Elton John sang Candle In The Wind; his tribute to Diana and as the clock struck 11am, the whole nation stood in silence for 2 minutes, while we said goodbye to our fair Englands Rose. Together as one, the nation bowed its head and mourned a beloved Princess.

After the service, the hearse began its 76 mile journey to Althorp. The roads lined with mourners, some waving their last farewell and throwing flowers along the way.

The very last stage began as the hearse carrying Diana's body, entered the gates of Althorp House and the Island that was to be her final resting place. The many thousands of flowers were gradually gathered together and taken there.

Throughout the year that followed, Diana was hardly out of the news headlines. Unseen before photographs, filled the daily newspapers and special magazines, tributes to Diana. They were a keepsake for all those who cared.

Speculation of whether it had been murder or accidental death continued; but no matter what the outcome and whether or not we will ever know the real truth, we cannot turn back the clock.

We lost a Princess whom we all loved, there is no doubt that she was indeed a special lady. Diana lifted the spirits and hearts of everyone she came into contact with and we could not fail to be moved as we witnessed the way she showed her concern for those who were in need. Her smile and gentle touch, meant so much to the average person in the street and these are the things she will be remembered for.

LIFE AFTER SALTS • 131

1997 Louisa Bennett places flowers of remembrance to Princess Diana

Althorp House opened its gates to the general public in July 1998. A museum was opened in Diana's memory, in which mementos of her life could be seen and those who wished to spend quiet moments in thought, were able to sit and view the Island where she lies at rest.

Who could have envisaged that the car crash in Paris would come so soon after Princess Diana's visit to Swadlincote in 1991 and among those who felt sad because of the news was Louisa Jane Bennett; she was the little girl chosen to present a bouquet of flowers to the Princess.

Louisa was thirteen in 1997, when she heard of the tragic loss of Princess Diana and she felt so sorry at what had happened that she sent a heartfelt message 'Our thoughts are with you' to Princess Diana's grieving sons, William and Harry.

At the Grove Hall memorial garden in Swadlincote, Louisa carefully placed a spray of flowers alongside the plaque commemorating Diana's wedding to Prince Charles and as the days followed and the world mourned, others in the town also laid their flowers, showing that they too felt the loss of a beloved Princess.

In Oct 1991, a news item, appeared in the Herald and Post. The picture showed the old Rink dance hall in the proceeds of being demolished to make way for new shops and business units. The caption spoke for itself. Demolition workers tearing down the Swadlincote Rink, had the job done for them in minutes, when fire swept across the site.

Firefighters believe small contractors fires started the blaze. They fought for almost two hours to extinguish it.

It really was a sad ending for something held in such high esteem by so many. Now all that's left of the Rink are the reunions that are held in its memory.

When the Rink dance hall caught fire, the old couples were standing round and they were saying - Swadlincote will never be the same and the lady who was crying at the bottom of Rink passage, 'course, when it was all over I said to 'er. "Neer mind me duck, you and I probably danced together years and years ago," and she said. "We probably did, but it'll never be the same again." I said. "You have a right old cry, you'll feel better."

We had a big reunion in February 1997. Eric Newbould organised that and we had it at the Greenbank Swad. There must have been about 250 people there. They could have sold double the tickets of the people who used to meet up at the Rink. It was a really good night. Rex McKay did the video of it, 'cause he does videos. Yes, it was really good to see a lot of those who used to go to the Rink; but the trouble was, you didn't recognise half of em, they'd got grey hair!

Bill began on Swadlincote Market in 1969, after selling a few rugs to friends. Within a couple of years he worked six markets a week, including two at Burton, two at Uttoxeter and best of all two at Swadlincote.

In 1973, the business moved into the old Primitive Methodist Chapel and Schoolroom, on the corner of Regent Street, Church Gresley, where it remained until 1984.

Once the markets began to decline in importance, Bill continued the long hours. In those days he was a salesman, measurer, estimator and carpet fitter rolled into one.

I used to work at the Rink dance hall in Swad 1955, in the cloakroom, with another lady named Cissy Hyman. The charge for looking after coats and shoes was tuppence in old money, and Ernie Hall, used to pay us ten shillings for working from 8 to 11pm on Saturdays. That was a lot of money then.

134 • INTO THE LIGHT 2000

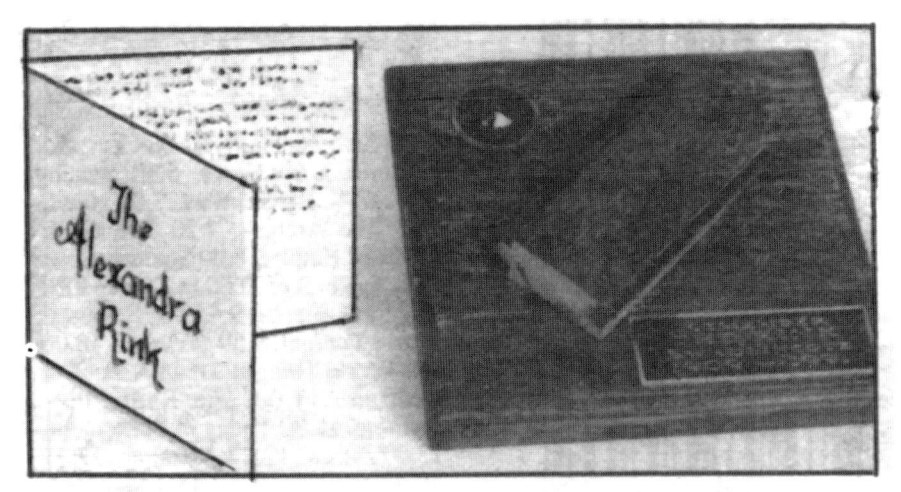

● The gift set . . . part of the dance floor.

The Rink Dance Hall, a piece of the famous floor

1999 Bill Toon

The business flourished and staff numbers increased, necessitating a move from the cramped premises at the Chapel, Toons carpets moved to a large showroom near Bonas at Castle Gresley. The Chapel remained in Bills hands however and was used as an opportunity to expand the scope of the business to include furniture.

The two businesses continued to flourish side by side for eight years. However, both businesses were beginning to outgrow their sites. Add the obvious economies of combining the two businesses and the solution was clear. Toons furniture would merge with Toons Carpets at the Castle Gresley site, where an extension would more than triple the current floor space.

The store now has the largest selection of carpets, rugs, furniture and curtains in the area and is also one of the largest independent stores in the country.

Bill's commitment to provide the best value, choice and quality in the area, has made Toons into a household name around Swadlincote, which is a fitting monument to his hard work over the last three decades.

Late October 1998, I was on the main road travelling towards Burton on Trent from Swadlincote, when the traffic almost slowed to a standstill.

I was in no particular hurry, but naturally, as the minutes ticked by and the traffic was still crawling along, my mind began to wonder what was causing the congestion.

It wasn't the time of year for caravanners, or harvesting time, so it wasn't a go slow tractor, but the one thing I would never have thought of was a Shelabier.

I hadn't seen one for a very long time, but this was Swadlincote and Shelabiers were a familiar sight years ago and here I was witnessing a part of that past entering into the present.

As the procession turned slowly to the right, I could see the black immaculate carriage, bearing the coffin, decorated with flowers and pulled by two jet black horses; their manes flowing in the wind and their coats glistening in the sunlight.

As the procession continued in a stately manner down the lane, I noticed that no one in the traffic queue, that now stretched backwards almost out of sight, seemed to mind having been held up for so long and no one was in a hurry to press on to rejoin the busy world. Perhaps, their minds, like mine, were with the family, who knew that their loved one was taking his or her last majestic ride on this beautiful earth of ours. No need to hurry things along. It was time to reflect.

Since a number of the old buildings in Swadlincote have gone, for instance, the Free Library in Alexander Road, lost through mining subsidence, doesn't it make you wonder who built some of them in the first place.

My Grandad, Charles Venning, was a builder and he was responsible for quite a lot of the buildings in Swadlincote.

He was helped by the fact that he had thirteen children, seven of which were boys and they helped him with his building projects.

He built Hastings Road School, York Road School, York Road Chapel, Hastings Road Chapel, The Old Library up Alexander Hill, also he built six houses at the top of Sandcliffe Road, Midway, Swadlincote and Grandad didn't stop there, he also built the Methodist Chapel at Hartshorne.

Coronation Street Swadlincote, was built in 1937 and the old Prince of Wales come here that year, to a place up Commonside there, in the Barley Mow; it was the out of work men's club, but it's Good Companions today. A chap named Master Redfern looked after that and his wife was a midwife.

The Street did well, it lasted until 1998, then like a number of other buildings around Swadlincote it finally succumbed to subsidence. The householders were eventually moved to other accommodation and the buildings themselves demolished.

I lived in Coronation Street for most of my life. It was a good place to live. All the neighbours were good, especially, if anyone was in trouble and if anyone along the street died, Elaine, my next door neighbour and myself, would go collecting from the other houses.

Everyone gave willingly and we would buy a wreath; any money left over went to the family.

Before I got married, I lived in the street. There was no electric light at first and we used Calor Gas, until the electric was installed.

We had our first TV for the Queen's Coronation. If you were one of the first to have a television, everyone came to watch.

The houses were big and very cold and as time went on, due to subsidence, they had to be propped up.

In about 1969, we had to move up to Midway, while the houses were made safe. After the repairs, we came back. This time to No 3, instead of No 5. Some neighbours stayed up there.

Years ago, no cars or caravans were allowed on the front gardens. The husband's were very good and would grow most of the family vegetables in the large back gardens. The women did the front gardens and took a pride in their flowers. On summer evenings, we would sit out on our back gardens, talking to one another many a time, 'til 11-O-Clock at night.

At one time, there was very little traffic, so the children could play out at football and other games.

Years earlier, when I lived with my parents in Coronation Street, one of my brothers, Walter Guest, owned a pony and kept it in fields off Coronation Street.

He bought it with money he had earned going coal picking at Boardman's Hill and selling it for half a crown a bag.

I can remember my dad and other men in the street, growing their vegetables in the long back gardens. There would be a competition each year, to see who had grown the biggest and best. There would be much activity caring for the growing produce with lots of smelly manure permeating the air, making it impossible to have the windows open.

The last tenants to move from the now demolished Coronation Street, were Mrs Galer, her three grown up children, two daughters and a son. They had to endure for five months, the trauma of empty houses being demolished all around them.

Mrs Galer, or Lillian as she is known, had been the first tenant to set up home in Coronation Street and had enjoyed living there. It had been handy for shops and her children found it handy for School.

The only drawback had been the coldness of the house, with only a fire in the living room; this was typical of many houses built by councils before the war.

Not only that, as time went on, like so many houses situated in a mining area, subsidence of the ground caused big structural problems to buildings. It was nevertheless very traumatic for the family. "I found it so frightening when the other houses were being pulled down," said Lillian. "Vandals would come along and break the windows. We had windows broken and once, someone got into the house. I lost my neighbours and got depressed and wouldn't eat; being in a wheelchair didn't help. Then on Friday the thirteenth of December last year, 1998, we had a letter telling us we were to move to Davis Road."

Debbie and Tracy who lived with their mum, talked about going to look at the house. There was a tremendous lot of work to do, as the new house had to be adapted to enable their mum to have access in and out.

On the twenty first of December, the family moved in. It was chaotic for Christmas. Clifford Galer, the son, said. "We aren't allowed to keep pigeons here, but it's nice to be living in a warm and dry house."

I wonder how many people can remember when there was a market in the Horse and Jockey yard at Newhall and Mrs Harvey used to fry fish and chips in an open fired chippy.
The Church bells used to ring every Sunday and as a girl at School, I remember the Catholic Church used to walk through Newhall in religious processions carrying different banners.

Bretby Hall is not at all like a hospital, but of course it wasn't built as one. It was a mansion, built in the time of James 1st, home of the Caenarvons. The most famous was the 5th Earl of Caenarvon who sponsored the expedition in Egypt to find King Tutankhamun's tomb. He it was, who with Howard Carter, was the first to set eyes on the wonders of the tomb in 1922.

The Tutankhamun 'legend' had it that the explorers would meet an untimely death. Howard Carter, leader of the expedition was the first. The death of the Earl caused speculation. Another legend associated with Bretby, concerned the Cedar of Lebanon which grew by the Hall. It was planted in 1676, but it is no longer there. Its heavy branches were protected by iron chains, to prevent any branches from falling, as this foretold the death of a member of the Caenarvon family. True or not, this tree was killed by the chains which were meant to save it.

In 1926, Bretby Hall was purchased by Derbyshire County Council for £26,000 and became an Orthopaedic Hospital of great renown. The surviving offsprings of the Cedars of Lebanon stand proudly, almost defiantly, around the Hall today.

I was privileged to be a patient in Bretby Hospital for an operation on my foot. Like many other patients I thought if the surgeon couldn't help me, the lovely surroundings would.

In the hospital

Early in the evening, the Sister was instructing the patients before they left for home; all except me. I had to stay for the night, because the toe in question wouldn't stop bleeding. "I shall have your bed moved into the next room for tonight," said Sister. "I don't want to stay in there all by myself when it gets dark," I said. "All the lights from the big windows will shine out on the lawns and I can't get up and walk, never mind run!"

"You'll be all right Mrs Harvey, you can have a tablet to alleviate the pain and it will help you to sleep."

I was pushed in my bed to that other big room and imagined all kinds of odd looking shadows. I heard animals making hideous noises through the dark night and thought I heard footsteps on the gravel paths. All alone, I wondered. Who? What? When? The pain in my foot subsided and I felt sleepy.

Bretby Hospital with Famous Cedar Tree

As dawn was breaking, I opened my eyes, but I daren't move and I couldn't speak. In the dim light, I saw a figure in a long white garment writing on a clipboard. I took a deep breath. "Oh No,I've died and gone to heaven," I thought and that's St.Peter filling in the details." I made murmurs and the figure turned to me. "How do you feel now Mrs Harvey?"

With a gasp, I answered. "Much better for hearing you." Sister laughed as I explained what I had thought earlier.

"How about a cup of tea then?" she said.

A number of years ago, I was working for a building contractor, as a bricklayer and we had to do some work at the Bretby Hospital. Whilst we were there, it was wintertime and very cold. We were working both indoors and outdoors on the actual hospital itself.

We used to get there about half past seven and as we arrived, I was amazed at what I saw. They were pushing the beds with all the youngsters in who obviously had very serious illnesses like tuberculosis and apparently, at that time, the doctors thought that fresh air was the thing for them.

Those poor children were put outside in freezing conditions and I remember that I and the fellows I was working with, we'd got the hot aches and many a time we were banging our hands and rubbing them together, trying to get them warm. I looked at those young children and thought, 'Well, here we are moaning, because we'd got the hot aches and yet those poor children had illnesses that were so bad, some of them couldn't even walk,' and it made me feel very sad and I thought how fortunate I was just to have the hot aches.

Something quite interesting happened while we were working there. We had to alter the Matron's office, which was in one of the big round turrets as it were and there was this big marble fireplace, an absolutely beautiful looking thing, it was and my boss said. "Now, I want you to take that fireplace out very carefully. We must save that." So, there were three of us working on it and we were taking it out very nicely, piece by piece, when we realised that it wasn't actually marble at all. It was slate and it had been made to look like marble. They did a lot of that many years ago.

We'd been at it for about an hour and a half, when the boss came back and said. "Ooh!" he says. "er, it doesn't matter now," he says. "er, you can smash it up and chuck it on the lorry." We said in amazement. "Are you sure!" and he says. "Ooh yes, yes. It's all right," he says. "I thought I'd got someone who wanted it, but no, he didn't in the end. It's not worth a lot and who could fit one of these in their homes," Well we understood what he meant, because it really was a massive fireplace.

So, what we did, we got a big hammer and we smashed it all up and the matron hearing the noise, suddenly came in and saw what we were doing. She was devastated and she says. "Oh no! that beautiful fireplace. I've sat here in this office for many years and that's been my pride and joy and now, you're smashing it up." Of course, we had to tell her why and then she insisted that we break a suitable piece off it as a memento for her to keep.

That was a sad story really, but nice that the Matron could have something special to remember her time there at Bretby Hospital, which she'd obviously enjoyed very much.

While there, working on the building, it was at a time when the famous Cedar Tree of Lebanon was still there, all chained up. The story, well known, that if a branch fell off, someone in the Caernarvon family would die. So the boughs had been chained up to stop them falling. But while we were there, it was decided by the powers that be, to take the tree down. Many people used to come and look at it, out of curiosity and those that saw it cut down, took small pieces home to remind them of the tree that had been there since it was first set, back in the 1600's.

These are some of the things I remember, that happened maybe in the late 50's, something like that, but when the Hospital closed, much later on, it certainly brought back a lot of memories for me.

Incidentally, during the second world war 1339-45, Bretby Hospital was used for a while to look after the British soldiers that were injured during the war. I had a sister named Joyce, who was working there at the time as a nurse and she'd said they were kept very busy. So, there's really quite a lot of history about Bretby Hospital, isn't there!

Just one of the miracles performed at Bretby Hospital. Baby Gordan Lowe, whose parents lived in Main Street, Newhall, about sixty years ago; was

We used to have a Town Crier come to Newhall, and he made a tour of every street, ringing his bell and reading announcements. That was before the use of radio. It was often through the Town Crier, that news of importance and National events first reached the villages. It was also for the benefit of those who couldn t read, or couldn t afford a newspaper. The last Town Crier, a man known as Paddy Watson, was killed in a Pit accident, and he was never replaced.

born with badly deformed feet. His mother carried him to Bretby Hospital, full of hope and faith and against the wishes of her family, begged the surgeon to help.

Several operations were duly performed and Gordan eventually, was able to walk. He and his wife became stars in the dancing world and many are the awards they received to prove it.

I met Gordan and his wife recently and we spoke of this.

When I was a junior, I used to like fishing. The first time I went, was to the top pond at Bretby. My mother came with me that day and we hadn't been there long when the fishing licence bailiff came along and, yes, I did have a permit.

I soon felt a fish bite and the float went right under, gradually, I hauled the catch towards the waters edge. My mum was panicking. "What shall we do when you land the fish?" she said. To be honest, I wasn't sure myself and we were the only people there. Just a couple of feet away from the waters edge, the fish emerged and then the hook broke and the fish lived to swim another day. We both gave a sigh of relief.

Next time I went, there were more experienced anglers with me and I caught a tench. Someone helped me to take the hook out and photographed me and we then returned the fish back to the pond.

A reminder of that legendary Cedar tree of Bretby, is in the hands of Arthur Staley of Winshill, whose family has many links with Bretby. Both his grandparents farmed there as tenants of the Earl of Caernarvon, under his late Uncle, Mr Harry Upton, who was a carpenter.

Mr Upton carved a cup from the wood of the tree when it was felled and the four inch high cup bears an inscription giving the date of the planting of the tree as 1646.

The snow was crisp beneath my feet,
as we made our way to the tree.
And the wind whistled round the pixie-
hood, that mum had made for me.

I was so excited, I tried to run fast,
along that icy track,
But I slipped and slithered and finally fell,
landing flat in the snow, on my back.

Dad lifted me high on his shoulders.
He often did that for me.
And we jogged along through the crisp white snow,
I was first to catch sight of that famous tree.

"Why are the branches chained, dad,
so they can't fall to the ground?"
"It's because of the curse on the family," he replied.
"When the tomb of King Tut was found."

"It was said, those who opened the tomb, would die,
when the branches fell from the tree."
My mouth opened wide and I gulped at the thought.
"Gosh dad! I'm glad that it wasn't me."

He laughed. "It's only an old wives tale," he said.
And it came from a long time ago."
And as he lifted me high on his shoulders,
the sky went dark and it suddenly began to snow.

As we jogged along, I just had to look back,
at that famous cedar tree.
And I shuddered at the thought of them opening the tomb.
And I was really glad, that it hadn't been me.

LIFE AFTER SALTS • 145

The Memorial Hall in Newhall has a fascinating history, which is also connected to another history of great interest to the Swadlincote people and indeed to the world.

The hall was built in 1874 and the inscription over the front door states, 'By Anne, Countess of Chesterfield, in memory of her dear son, George 7th Earl of Chesterfield and it further states 'the only son of his mother and she a widow' (the 7th Earl contacted scarlet fever and died).

The Hall cost £3,000 and upstairs is a large room with a minstrel gallery.

The hall was opened by Lord Carnaervon and here is where the Tutankhamun connection lies.

Lord Carnaervon owned much of the land in the nearby Bretby area. He was an Egyptologist and has a place in history. Together with Howard Carter at Luxor in 1992-3, they discovered the tomb of King Tutankhamun; a King in Egypt of the 18th dynasty, about 1350BC. The mummy was intact and the tomb full of priceless treasures.

Another land mark in the area of
Swadlincote - has closed.
Built just outside the town,
away from the smoke and dusty
part of Swad that was yesteryear.
Up and over the hill, amongst woods
and fields and lakes full of fish.
So beautiful a place, that even now,
makes one hold the breath, and
want to stay there forever.
Its past once linked with Tutunkhamun,
and the legend of the famous Cedar tree
of Lebanon.

This treasured landmark was once known as
BRETBY HALL.

Get your skis on

As the years passed by, I watched with great pleasure as the hole that turned out to be (Wraggs and Woodwards Clay workings) was gradually filled in and the blackness turned green as it eventually became carpeted with grass and lined with trees.

Then along came Tony Freeman and had it all dug up again. Tony, had obviously been watching over the years and ideas were forming in his head. Already an accomplished skier himself, he could see what the shape and location of the filled in opencast clay workings could be changed into.

Having a good imagination, Tony visualized a Dri Ski Slope there and with the help from Mark Butler and others, he turned his ideas into reality.

Tony was the first to see the Dry Ski Slope as a training centre, not only for those who liked to spend their holidays ski-ing down the slopes of mountains in Switzerland etc., but to make good skiers of those who cannot get to the real thing. Then Tony went a step further and tried to hint at the real thing by providing a mountain atmosphere, not only on the slopes, but in the restaurant, with Apple Strudel on the menu and a real log fire to create the smell of wood smoke.

International downhill skier, Martin Bell, put Swadlincote on the Sporting map when he opened the town's £750,000 dri Ski Slope, at a champagne reception in October 1987. He described the development as one of the finest sporting facilities in the midlands. Later on, a Toboggan run was added and for more than 10 years, it has been a tremendous success.

Whoever thought that Swadlincote would be in the forefront of providing such a wonderful facility. Too late for some of us perhaps, with regard to actually putting on skis and heading down the Piste. It would be far too risky for delicate old bones. What is it that they say in Show Business, as the performers go on stage - 'Break a leg'

In the course of time, Tony moved on and the John Nike Leisuresport Ski Centres added Swadlincote to their list of Ski centres at Bracknell, Chatham and Plymouth and Swadlincote then became the Premier Artificial Skiing facility in the midlands.

If you stand at the top of the ski slope, and look down, out across Swad, and you look at the new sort of street decorations, as they'd call em along the High street, and up round the delph, I always envisage myself, standing at the top of the ski slope, with a giant marble, and rolling it down, because the view from there looks like a pinball machine. It can bounce up and down, and I think they ought to have put lights on top of them posts, it just looks like a pinball machine all lit up.

I went up to see them one day, taking with me, a wartime evacuee, who was on a nostalgic trip, remembering back to the time when, as a very young girl she was evacuated from the City of London, to Hartshorne village in Derbyshire.

Brenda also being an accomplished skier herself, I had promised that we would pay the Ski Centre a visit.

We sat in the covered glass veranda, drinking coffee, watching the skiers on the slope and reminiscing about the days of the war.

"Swadlincote is different now, from how I remember it in 1944," said Brenda. "It was a bit of a dingy place back then and I should think it was from all the potteries working, throwing out fumes and smoke. But now, it's a clean place. There's lots more greenery everywhere and although Swadlincote is not a large town, it's wonderful to have a ski centre here. It should bring in tourists from miles around. When I come over again for another visit, I might bring my own skis and try it out."

It was a memorable day for both of us and I had been truly impressed by the caring attitude and warm hospitality of the Ski Centre. There is indeed much enjoyment to be had there for would be skiers.

There is a separate Nursery slope which ensures that teaching can take place without interruption and it helps those who lack confidence to feel more assured.

The Toboggan Run, with its 650m descent, winds its way down and around the ski slopes and is the only one of its kind in the midlands and is popular with everyone, in particular children, who seem to thrive on excitement. They think it's marvellous.

Snowboarding is well established now on the winter sports scene, with a worldwide recognition as the new sport on snow. Mind you, watching it on television, it amazes me how they can do so many twists and turns, not counting the effortless somersaults. Alright, you've guessed it! I'm only jealous and wish I was back in my teens.

The Centre is also very popular for celebrations of all kinds and of course in the winter, a blazing log fire adds to the warmth of the Centre's hospitality.

In 1997, the Ski Centre celebrated its 10th Anniversary and over those years, many thousands of ski beginners have passed through its doors to become recreational skiers, thanks to the dedicated team of teaching professionals.

In 1998, the renovated Swadlincote Ski Centre's main slope of 160m was completed and the regular visitors and Ski Club members all agree that is was worth waiting for.

The Centre, always ready to move with the times, has begun preparation for a Snowboard Park! and now, with Swadlincote's new image - no smoke - no grime, what a tremendous view there is also to enjoy from the top of the main slope.

What wouldn't we have given 50 odd years ago, for this wonderful sporting facility in Swadlincote, but for us who where born to soon, they were only dreams.

LIFE AFTER SALTS • 149

1999 On the piste. Swadlincote Ski Centre

History in the Making

Yee Ha!

What was once our High Street, is now a shopping centre.
Everywhere is pedestrianised, where vehicles can't enter.
At least, that's what the signs say, that are up there for people to see.
But them in cars are short sighted, well it seems that way to me.
There's more cars in town with orange stickers than you could ever guess,
and there's me trying to get out of the way, I get in such a mess.

They've made some little flower beds and filled them with plastic trees.
"Count your blessings" I was told "There's no pollen to make you sneeze."
All the old shops have gone. There was once th' 'Nags Head'
Now pulled down and in its place we've a super market instead.
Do you want a greetings card? We've a dozen shops, all with fancy prices.
Take your pick, there's plenty. Can't say which is the nicest.

In spite of all this modernization the people will never alter,
We're proud us folk from Derbyshire and our pride will never falter.
We're proud to meet up with our friends and put the world to right.
Make naughty remarks about folk passing by "Goodness - What a sight!"
We look around, scratch our heads. Often long for things that have long since gone.
But the young ones say this is progress, so we just have to carry on.

But we're proud of our traditions and will keep our memories of the past.
The shops and signs will chop and change. But our heritage will always last.

Everybody knows that market traders are very hardy people and they used to manage in winter on the delph, with the flares and hot mugs of tea for warmth.

Most of them are gone now and we sometimes wonder, will there ever be another Lenny Blankly, or another family like the Harrison sisters, described as amazon women, because they could do anything - drive lorries and lift sacks of potatoes like any man; they were legends in their own time. But even if we never have anyone to replace them, each generation that comes, will have its own characters.

Even now, we have the next generation of market traders in the covered in market built in 1984. They have become stalwarts in their own right.

Dorothy Smith has been a market trader for a long time, 35 years in fact and she remembers what it was like on the delph, with all the hustle and bustle and she remembers too, the long hours they all worked, often till Nine O Clock at night. Her husband was with her on the stall then, until he died.

Dorothy's parents ran the business in the 1920's and when they retired, Dorothy carried the business on and is still going.

Over the years, she has made a lot of friends, who have become her 'regulars' and they always look forward to seeing her smiling face.

The younger market traders, like Simon Wardle at the Pet stall, always seems to be rushed off his feet and Peter at P and L Meats, who has been in the top corner of the market for 3 years, both agree that it is the regulars who continually give their steady support that keeps them going.

Keith Oakey, on the curtain stall, has been a market trader for 14 years in Swadlincote, so he's seen quite a few changes. Di, his young daughter, works on the stall next to him, with bags and handbags of all kinds and between them they're a good team.

Soon, we may have a surprise in our forward looking town of Swadlincote. The French company, Market Initiatives, which assumed managerial control of the covered in market in April 1999, has a plan to establish up to a 20 stall market back on the delph and a collectors flea market in the Town Hall, which will compliment our already established market traders. That will be sure to put a smile on the faces of the old timers!

Young girls often used to go straight from school into 'Service' and there was a Mrs Reeves who had an agency for Domestic Servants. General maids: House parlour maids: Nurses and in between maids, in various parts of the country. The wages were £30. £20.£18, down to £10 - that wouldn't have been bad if it was for a week, but that was for a YEAR.

HISTORY IN THE MAKING • 153

MARKET TRADERS

1999 Peter P&R Meats

1999 Simon Wardle Pet Shop

154 • INTO THE LIGHT 2000

MARKET TRADERS

1999 Keith Oakley and Di his daughter

1999 Dorothy Smith

Swadlincote in the 90's is beginning to spread its wings, to accommodate some of the new superstores. When they first opened their doors in the town in the 80's, after Salts had closed, we never thought we'd get used to the different way of shopping, but time has gone by and we have got used to it and it will be good to see others make their way over this side of Burton bridge.

Swadlincote can now boast a Sainsbury's, which is a delight to visit, there are so many things we've never tried before, like the exotic fruit for instance and the many different kinds of bread etc. and with Home Electric next door, you haven't got far to go for a new television, or a new cleaner, that is, if you can drag the other half away from watching the football on television at home.

I had good reason to see what the shop could offer me recently. I own a Labrador dog. He's a wonderful companion, but getting on a bit now and when he's moulting, which is most of the time, I end up with a wine coloured carpet that ends up looking like a white mowhair one. I've cleaned it to lose the static and used a brush that's supposed to collect the hairs. I've even gone over it with sellotape bit by bit, but nothing makes any difference and over the years, I've even changed cleaners three times, but always ended up disappointed.

Then one night, at a friend's house, they showed me their new cleaner, I was more than impressed with its performance, but THEY hadn't got a dog, so the next day, I walked into the shop, spotted one like it and said. "Does this cleaner remove dog hairs." The sales assistant looked at me and without flinching, she said. "Yes, madam." "I'll take it then," I said. "But if you're wrong, I'll bring it back tomorrow." I thought that will make her quake at the knees, but she just smiled nicely at me and handed me a large box with a child's cleaner in it to match the one I'd just bought. "You get this with it - free madam," she said.

'What a good offer,' I thought and although I didn't have any children, I knew someone who did and was able to make a little girl very happy.

That evening, with bated breath and honestly not much hope, I used the new fancy cleaner and Hey Presto! I couldn't believe my eyes. I now have a wine coloured carpet, at last. So, there's something to be said for progress after all, isn't there!

Christmas time was a bit different to what it is in Swad today. They couldn't just switch the lights on then, because they were lit by gaslamps. A man had to go round with a pole and light each lamp. The gas was manufactured down Belmont Street and was stored in a big holder somewhere near to where Somerfields is now. To add to the light from the gaslamps, all the shop windows were lit up, and the people were there till after 9pm, because they had been waiting for another pay day.

The shop of Scraggs Chemist in Swadlincote, is an olde worlde shape. It has a very high pointed roof and black beams on the front of the building, which we usually associate with earlier centuries, but the date on the building is 1930AD.

When I was a youngster, I would often stand outside the building and look at the coloured liquid in the big glass bottles in the window and often wondered what it was and what it tasted like. I'm never going to ask anyone, because it will spoil my childhood memory.

I always knew it then as Scraggs Chemist and it remained so, until 1987. Up to then it was owned by the family of Mr and Mrs Scragg, but with the death of Mr Scragg, it changed hands and Dean and Smedley took it over.

Later, they moved into larger premises in Swadlincote and in 1998, the building changed again and became St Giles Hospice Shop.

Boots Chemist is another shop that has been in Swadlincote for many years and happily is still with us. There are of course other shops of long standing and we acknowledge them all and hope they will remain with us many years into the future.

I had often wondered where Cloverleaf T.G.Green was situated and one day, I had occasion to search for them. We were tracing up some of the family, where they'd moved to and settled. My husband's father died when he was only six years old, so he couldn't remember what his dad looked like, but as we followed the road past Church Gresley Memorial gates and just over the rise, where the girdy bridge used to be, we drove up the lane on the left and there was the factory shop well signposted.

As we got out of the car, Bob said. "My dad used to work here at TG Green years ago, in the factory, when he came over here from Stoke on Trent, to live in the Swadlincote area.

I hadn't realised our trip was going to turn out to be a nostalgic one, so I left him for a while with his memories, as I entered the shop.

I've got to admit, I just don't know how it is possible to live in an area for 50 odd years and still miss a treasure like (Cloverleaf) TG Green's shop. Brenda Maddock the shop manageress and Jill Jacobs, the personnel officer were proud of their heritage and were happy to show me the famous Cornish ware range.

1999 Jill Jacobs, personnel officer. Brenda Madock, Factory shop Manageress.

Just as the coal mines have gradually closed down, we have also lost most of the pottery works in the Swadlincote area.

There used to be Sharpes Pottery, Thos:Wragg and Sons, Tooths pottery and Aults pottery; all of them enjoyed popularity in their day.

All gone now, but one Pottery firm is still going strong. TG Green, now Cloverleaf TG Green, in Church Gresley and has been going for more than 200 years and their pottery is still as popular as ever.

They still manufacture the traditional grit stand mixing bowls, as well as the famous Cornish Blue range, with its distinctive blue and white stripes, which represented the sky and waves of the cornish coast and was produced as far back as 1926.

The pieces are unique, because they are still turned by hand, using the same method when they were first introduced. The Cornish ware has now become very collectable and subsequently, its value has risen. Antique collecting has become very popular in the 90's and its always exciting when something turns up that was made in one of our potteries here in the Swadlincote area.

*In those days of
Rock n Roll,
just pre the Beatles,
all this modern sort of
standing about, shaking your
arms around.
We did a lot of jiving,
but there was part of
the evening, that you weren't allowed to
jive at the Rink,
and we had to do the
Palais Glide -
It was a bit like
Line Dancing.*

When the Rink dance hall in Swadlincote closed down, the local dancers seemed to be in a sort of limbo as to where to go. Dinner and dance was the option, but of course that was too expensive to do every week, so many of us gave up looking for a place to go.

Disco dancing was only for the young. But have you noticed how things have a habit of coming round again, like the new style cinemas in the 90's. People are gradually being coaxed out of their armchairs and spending family nights out together. Also we have tea dances, where ballroom and sequence dancing are enjoyed by everyone.

Time continues to move on and now, there's a style of dancing that anyone can do and it's very much alive in Swadlincote.

Have you donned YOUR cowboy hat and boots. Yee Hah! Come on down to Castle Gresley with Ian and Sue Gregory, at the Victory Club twice a week. Mondays and Wednesdays 8pm. They will show you how to strut your stuff and have a real good time.

Then there's the Grove at the Leisure Centre. Klara McDonald has been fourteen times and in her own words - "It's great fun. I love it. You don't need a partner; it's something you can do on your own and when the children come to the beginners class at 7-8pm." she said, laughing. "You want to sit and watch them for a bit and you'll find out that they know more than you do. The Texan Rangers are there at 8-15pm to 10pm and they all wear the cowboy gear. They really look great.

Another couple who started line dancing about two years ago, was Joan and Walter White. They went to a room against the Gresley Park, where Ian and Sue Gregory first started classes for line dancing.

At that time Sue worked at Bretby Orthopedic Hospital.

"Ian's a very good teacher," said Joan, "and wouldn't go on until you were sure of the steps. It's great exercise and good, because it's something you can do on your own, so, those who have lost their husband or wife, don't have to feel out of it, because they too can join in.

Walter, Joan's husband, always ready for a laugh or two, used to show Jenny and Wendy, friends of theirs, how to do a few steps of line dancing, but part way through, he would always go wrong, deliberately, well - that's what he said it was. anyway!

Another venue for line dancing is Gresley Old Hall. Just over two and a half years ago, aerobics teacher Shirley Pickess, started line dancing classes. At first she said she wasn't prepared for the huge response and her special dancing nights at the Burton Town Hall attract hundreds of people from all over the Midlands.

Shirley believes in line dancing in style. The dress she is wearing in the photograph by Ken Nichols, is a Pink top and skirt in 4 layers and the outfit is completed by the Cowboy boots and white Stetson.

Alan, a former Rock N Roll dance champion, attended Shirley's first class and has been a regular ever since. He has his wife Mary, to thank for his customised western style shirts.

Chestnut Valley Rebels is the name of Shirley's group. The U.S style makeover, transformation was by courtesy of Tracey Smith.

HISTORY IN THE MAKING • 161

1998 Alan Hodgkins with Shirley Pickess, Line Dance Teacher

Having become a member of St.John's Church in the 1950's, I heard that Eileen Harvey was directing a pantomime for the children and popped in at a rehearsal of 'Mother Goose.' She got me to read the Witch's part and eventually asked me to do it, though I'd really only meant to bring in my children.

"Witch, eh? Thank you, Eileen, me darlin,' now I know what I really look like," I giggled.

"Nothing to do with that," she protested, "you've made your voice sound so old and haggish like..." Ah well, that was a bit better so I forgave her.

My children were welcomed with open arms and all three had parts in the pantomimes and, not to be outdone, so did my husband. Lots of mothers helped with the costumes and all the numerous things that have to be done, but Eileen has always known how to deal with children.

I can't remember many of the children's names and I think that Eileen is now a bit hazy, but I do remember doing a song and dance on stage with the hilarious Horace Pickering to the tune of 'Takes two to Tango' and a threesome with him and Trevor Greaves singing 'Nobody Loves a Fairy When She's Forty'. What fools we looked, all with broken wands dressed up in glitter and stars and frills. The men in drag nearly brought the house down. How we enjoyed it! Eileen had some brilliant ideas.

The poor lady 'did her nut' from time to time with all the hard work entailed, but her pantomimes were always a success and a help to church funds. In subsequent years, she also produced 'Cinderella' and 'The Sleeping Beauty,' The children loved it.

Children of today could never imagine a life without television, or computers, but years ago we always had so much to do, life was never boring. Amateur dramatic societies were part of community life. Churches and Chapels were always expected to 'put something on ' in the winter. A Pantomime, Play, or Concert in the Spring.

Scripts were never brought in for the Pantomimes. Everybody knew the traditional Panto stories by heart, all that was needed to add was dialogue and a few popular songs to get the audience singing. Most families had a piano in those days and at least one in the family knew how to play, so there was never any shortage of a pianist. Rehearsals kept us busy most weekends and nights,

HISTORY IN THE MAKING • 163

1951 T Greaves, Pat Cowlishaw, H Pickering, Mother Goose production

up to the day of production. There was always a lot of excitement and whatever we staged was appreciated by all and usually on the last day of the production, nearly always someone would ask - What are you doing next year!

*Some years ago was written a song
to do with fairies who were long
in the tooth with face less fair,
eyes less bright and losing hair,
who've lost the art of being naughty
Christmas Fairies over forty.*

*And here's me on this Christmas tree,
I've reached the age of forty three.
Cracked wand in hand up here I stand
for several weeks with leg that creaks.
One arm gone, one blue eye missing,
dress that's torn and only wishing
I were packed up in my box again,
for now I cannot stand the strain
of trying to look sporty
now that I'm a fairy over forty.*

*To tell the truth I'v had enough
they need a younger bit of stuff.
Oxfam, I'm sure, would turn me down,
up here I'm feeling such a clown.
Looking daft instead of haughty
now I'm a fairy over forty.*

Swadlincote's stars

The last chapter in our book, is devoted to our painters, musicians and the amazing talent of Swadlincote's up and coming stars of stage, screen and radio.

I've always had the urge to paint, but I've not always had the opportunity.

When I was a pupil at Ashby Girls Grammar School, our Art teacher didn't spend a lot of time with us as first years. She came to the class and brought a sheet which she threw over the blackboard and carefully made folds in it. Then she told the class. "This will be your subject for this half term.

"I want everyone of the creases shown in your sketches as folds. Light and dark pencil shading please." Thirty girls all sighed together and the teacher was not at all pleased.

We had lovely views from each window in the room, but she said firmly. "No - draw the sheet." All the beautiful flowers were in bloom, but NO - Draw the sheet. Pupils scattered about the room would have made good models, again it was No, Draw the sheet. What a waste of talent, time and pencil lead.

Many years after leaving Ashby Girls Grammar School, I remembered it all. I still wanted to paint, so I joined a class for adults at the Pingle School in the 50's.

It was a joy. All the men and women wanted to paint. I still have one of the paintings my husband did. He was teased about the number of leaves, but it's a great painting.

Later, I joined a class at my old school in Winshill. The tutor was happy, students were happy and we got on fine.

Then suddenly, the tutor left and we had four men tutors in four consecutive weeks.

The first one put out three empty wine bottles. "I want you to draw these," he said.

The next week, number two set out the bottles. "I want you to draw these," he said.

"What again!" I ventured.

By the third week I was ready to scream. "We did all that at school," I said.

When little Peck used shout Mercury on the Delph at Swad, although he was small in stature, his voice used to carry well as he shouted out the headlines of the newspaper. He would pick out the bits of news that he thought would sell the paper. One very cold wintry day, he was shouting at the top of his voice. "Big fire at Woodville," and the sale of the Mails, which had been flagging that day, suddenly began to pick up. One man who bought a mail said. "Where's that fire you were shouting about?" "It's at our house," said little Peck, "and the sooner I sell these Mails, the sooner I get to sit in front of it." - That's initiative for you.

"We haven't come to draw bottles." The class was in an uproar.

"Next week, bring your own specimen; Paper and paint!" he said.

I took a small sample of blue flowers, to put in the yellow vase I'd carried. The tutor said he didn't like the yellow vase and would I try to cover it in red. I went home in a very bad mood.

I took out my new canvas, which had been a christmas present and I painted the whole surface with a very dark brown oil paint. My husband stood there aghast. "What on earth...!" he said. "That was expensive!"

When it was dry I took it along to the art class.

"What are you going to do with THAT!" said the tutor.

I surprised him by painting a bunch of Chinese Lanterns during the next four weeks. The orange globes on the dark background looked fantastic!

Like many folk who want to paint. WE know what we want even if others don't.

I've reduced the number of finished paintings that I've got at home now. If anyone comes and says. "I like that," I make them a gift of the painting. After all I don't need so many now. Do I. I'll soon be 85!

I didn't start painting until about a year after my husband Hubert, died. It was strange really. I was 74 and at the Chapel that I go to, there was an Art class and one of the ladies said to me. "Why don't you come," and although I'd never done any painting at School or anywhere, because I was never any good at it. I found that when I got there, I could do it.

As the years have gone by, I've improved and I feel that it's been a gift from God for me, so always when I paint my pictures, the signature goes on of the fish, which is the sign of christianity and that always goes on, because I feel it has been a gift from him.

It has broadened my life. I've made so many friends and it has been a wonderful thing for me. I don't really know what I actually would have done without it. I've loved every minute of it and always say a prayer before I start painting, that this will be good and sometimes, after I've done it, I really can't believe that I'm the one who has actually done it.

Painting has also opened doors for me, because with the Art class now, I can go out. We have little trips you know and I can go out with them and it has

The Fairs seem to come all year round in Swadlincote these days. I'm not complaining mind, I love to see them, but haven't some of the rides changed. The mind boggles as I stand there watching them go round, or up and down, and even inside out. The rides we used to go on years ago were positively slow in comparison.

I think the moonrocket was probably the fastest then, and the horse carousel was fine if dad was holding tight to his son or daughter, sitting in front of him on the same horse. Then we had the chair o planes, that usually meant another curling iron job when you got home. Well, some of these have become collectors items now. Anyway, I'm content with just watching these days, I don't fancy my brains being scrambled.

made other friends for me, so that's been really good.

I still go to my painting class on a Tuesday mornings and I look forward to it. Then sometimes, in the wintertime, if the light is good, I can sit and paint and the hours just pass by and honestly, I can't believe how many hours have gone by; your mind focuses on it that much. Sometimes, when I'm painting a picture - like a cottage, I can almost feel as if I've been inside the cottage.

I don't always have to choose a subject myself to paint; someone will come along and bring me a card with a picture on and ask if I can make a painting of it. Or, I may choose a picture out of a book that I have, like the one on the wall. That one is Chatsworth House and the one over the fireplace, is a battle ship scene on the water, you can see where the cannon ball had dropped into the sea. It's got the stars and stripes on, because it's an American ship. I really enjoyed that one.

I've painted Bretby Hall seven times, for the nurses. I suppose they wanted something to remember it by, since it closed. I painted the building from a postcard, but I made it much bigger and I did it in the Autumn when the ivy leaves on the building were red.

I would certainly encourage elderley people to take up painting. it is a thing that you can sit and relax with. I mean, this chair's all built up with cushions, so that I can sit in the window and do it. I'm 78 now and I've still got my eyesight and can still hold paint brushes and things like that. It has all been a God send to me.

The History of the Newhall Brass Band can be traced back to the turn of the century and used to practise in the Church Army Hall in Main Street, Newhall, but in 1939, when the second world war broke out, a lot of the players were called up and the band had to be disbanded.

Later in time, it was decided to start the band up again, but by then the instruments were all over the place and when they were found, they were all black, in need of cleaning and some repair. However, the band carried on and in the 1950's began entering competitions again.

The success of the band with its association in 1970, with Ernest Woodhouse (FTCL.FVCM.LGSM.LTCL. (T)BBCM) who conducted from the age of fourteen.

The band reached championship status and during this successful period was

168 • INTO THE LIGHT 2000

1999 Dorothy Gough

1999 Newhall Brass Band. Concert work in the North East Midlands Association, they won their section. Back row. Left to Right: Peter Woodings, E Ford, Mrs J Ford, L Barnes, Pat Woodings, R Watson, K Unwin, J Fern, L Gould, N Merrick. Middle Row. Left to Right: D Harlow, E Fields-Pattinson, J Adey, B Morris, H Whitburn, M Pattinson, Alf Stevenson, K Ottowall, B Lucas. Front Row. Left to Right: D Lucas, T Clay, D Riley, D Walker, S Gittins, J Mason, A Morris, C Clulow, P Marklou.

fortunate in obtaining sponsorship from Burton Constructional Engineering and Webb Ivory Ltd.

During 1991, the economic depression and lack of finance, together with the reduction in playing members, precipitated a move from Newhall to free accommodation in Burton on Trent, provided by a local Publican, but in 1994, with the assistance of the Headmaster of Newhall Junior School, the band returned to Newhall and is now able to use the Memorial Hall for practise sessions.

The band has gone from strength to strength and in 1997, has been promoted from the fourth section to the third section, after coming in second from the competition held at Nottingham. There are twenty five players in the band and some of them have been playing a good many years.

On Sunday mornings at the Memorial Hall, - a school is run for youngsters who would like to be band players. This will ensure that the Newhall Brass Band will carry on for many years into the future.

One late afternoon as I got out of the car, after a ride in the country, I heard the sound of the accomplished players of the Newhall Brass Band; They were holding me transfixed with their haunting melodies, when I should have been in the kitchen preparing tea and feeding the dog. Then I began to wonder about the children of today. Are they encouraged to play such instruments? and my search began in earnest to find our young musicians in the area.

The first one I met was Emily Zara and this is what she said. "I'm eleven years old. I like music and I'm being taught how to play a Woodwind Clarinet, by Norman's the instrument shop at Burton on Trent, so I can play it at school with the school band.

I'm the only one at school who plays a Woodwind Clarinet. I don't think I want to be in a band when I grow up, I'd like to be a doctor to help people, but then I might change my mind again when I'm older.

We have a teacher at the Newhall Junior school. Her name is Miss Hathoway and she organised a trip to London for children to see Starlight Express and Oliver; they were very nice and we all enjoyed it.

After talking with Emily, I met her younger brother Daniel, who is ten years old. Daniel is being taught at school to play a Tenor Horn. He did say that he really wanted to play a Cornet, but the teacher gave him the Tenor Horn to play.

"Miss Beck comes in to teach us," he said, "and sometimes she gets a bit annoyed, because I don't practise enough."

"I was like that when I was learning to play the piano Daniel," I said. "In fact, most children try to get out of practising when they're very young. It's much more fun to go out and play."

Daniel is going to carry on learning to play the Tenor Horn. He doesn't want to be in a band, at least he doesn't think so, but he might change to another instrument as he gets older.

When I left him, I thought that whatever young Daniel did, he would do well, because not only does he play a fine instrument, he also has a highly creative side to his nature. He makes weird and wonderful models and is very familiar with the art of decoupage.

My name is Katy Storie. I'm thirteen and I play the Tenor Horn. My sister Becky plays the Cornet and I wanted to play an instrument, but not the same as her.

We both go to William Allit school,and it's only just over the road, so we don't have far to go. I go with Becky to the Memorial Hall on Sunday mornings and Des Boddice teaches us how to play. There's a boy named Mathew goes and Richard, but he's a lot younger.

I would like to play in the brass band, even when I'm older and perhaps win competitions,but I'm already in the junior band. We play Hymns and sea shanties.

My name's Becky Storie and I'm twelve. I go to the William Allit school at Newhall and one morning I saw Andrew Draycott, he's a boy at our school and he's about eleven or twelve. He brought a Cornet (musical instrument) to school to play it at Assembly and he was showing the class playing it and he told me where I could learn to play one.

The Newhall Brass Band runs a school on Sunday mornings at the Memorial Hall and Des Boddice teaches us how to play an instrument. I chose to play the Cornet. I'd like to play in the brass band, so I go on Sunday mornings to learn.

HISTORY IN THE MAKING • 171

1997 Left to Right:
M Pattinson, Richard, Michelle, Becky Storie, Sarah, Katy Storie

Left to Right:
Melissa Howard, Mathew, Michelle, Lois Print, Jessica Eley

There are about five others go as well. My sister Katy goes. We have a school band as well, but Mr Smith takes that.

Not long ago, some things were stolen from the Memorial Hall and instruments as well. Me mum saw what looked like one of the instruments in the shop up the road.

She went in and asked how much it was and then she told me she thought it was stolen and we'd see if it was like the one that belonged to the band and we found out that it was. It wasn't the Cornet that I played, but it was one of the bands instruments and they managed to get it back.

I climbed the stairs of the Memorial Hall in Newhall, Swadlincote, to meet the young children practising their brass band instruments, with a view to being our young banders of tomorrow, and as the music drifted down through the great Hall, I quickened my steps. It was so exciting and I was eager to meet the children.

I opened the door quietly, not wanting to disturb them too much and stood there thrilled to see youngsters with so much enthusiasm for the musical sounds they were creating. It was indeed a very pleasant experience listening to them.

When they stopped, I walked forward and introduced myself.

Music has always played a large part in the district and it has produced some of the best singing voices and bands. Certainly, the local people have good reason to be proud of their achievements past and present.

The first little boy I spoke to was very shy, but that wasn't surprising, he was only six years old and had a fit of the giggles. "His name is Richard," whispered the teacher, Michael Pattinson. I asked Richard what his other name was, but he said he didn't know; he was having me on of course, so I tried for - "Which instrument are you playing Richard?" and he whispered "A Cornet."

Michelle, the next little girl in the group and Becky Storie were also playing a Cornet. Sarah Elliot and Katy Storie were playing a Tenor Horn.

As I crept downstairs, the children were sitting, waiting for me, well, I had promised to photograph them in action, when they'd chosen a piece to play.

I moved carefully between each music stand, visualising the chaos that would follow if the stands with their arranged music on each one, were to be knocked over.

The first youngster was Jessica Eley from Newhall. Then I met Lois Print. She was playing a Cornet and another Michelle was also playing a Cornet. Next to Michelle was another little boy aged six years. His name was Mathew and on the end of the group was Melissa Howard, she was thirteen, the eldest.

At that point, the children all began talking among themselves. They were ready to play something for me and at the same time upstairs, the other children also began to play, so we had a mixture of Twinkle Twinkle Little Star, with whatever was being played upstairs. It all went down very well though.

I met Kelly, a young woman teacher replacing someone who was ill that day.

Jessica then took the lead and played God Save The Queen, on her own, followed by Michelle, Lois and Jessica playing When The Saints Go Marching In. It certainly was an exciting morning.

Gresley has had its male voice choir for many successful years and in 1997, they launched out on something new - a Boys Choir.

In one of the Concerts that year of 97, it brought together the combined talents of the Gresley Male Voice Choir, Ilfracombe Male Voice Choir and gave audiences a first taste of the new Gresley Boys Choir.

The Concert proved to be a great success. Mike Powell, a spokesman for the Gresley Male Voice Choir, said. "The Concert went really well and the boys choir went down a treat. What we are trying to do is give the boys a grounding in the tradition of male voice choirs, in the hope that they will come back and join the full choir when they are older.

The Gresley Boys Choir draws on the talents of youngsters age between 7-13 and the choir should do well, for the musical director, Roy Davies, was the former conductor of the famous Gresley Male Voice choir.

1999 Gresley Boys Choir. Back row. Left to Right: Mark Hadfield, Peter Robinson, Jonathon Hines, Peter Sharp, Simon Baldwin, Adam Swindell, Steven Hodgett.
Second row: Gerald Rogers, Accompanist. Daniel Andrews, Thomas Bennett, Liam Bowskill, Christopher Scanlon, Robert Salmon, Philip Morton, Roy Davies, Musical Director.
Third row: Joseph Wilde, Karl Dutton, Jonathon Moore, Jason Rose, Thomas Rankin, Damion Cope.
Front row: John Kreft, Sammy Hines, Chistopher Moore, Timmy Robinson, Christopher Boswell, Sean Shuttleworth, James Adams.

1997 Pingle School Big Band.
Back row, from the top: S Walker, S Freeman, R Sayer, M Smith, Keyboard M Power, Guitar J Wallews, Drummer D Lawley.
Left row, from the top: B Ricketts, C Frost, E Harrison, L Finch, S Worker.
Right row, from the top: S Gibson, J Cain, David Wiliams, J Harper, D Reid.
Front row: C Lang, N Tomlinson.

"Eh up Flo, I enner seen yo for years."

"No, I'n lived abroad that's why, but I'n com back to live in Swad now. Do yo live in the same place; that whate cottage along 'earthcote road?" "Arr," said Dora. "Ow about yo?" "I'm in one o them new fangled 'ouses a bit afore ya get to your place." "They enner got much garden, en they," said Dora. "No, none of the new ens en. That's why we 'ave to buy them freezers to put the stuff in."

"I enner got one," said Dora."

"No! cos you'n got a big garden, that's why. Does your Fred still set it wi taters and stuff?" "Arr.I'n just took me sister Francis some."

"I 'ave to stock up me freezer from shops," said Flo. That's where I'n bin todee."

The two friends walked along the High street in Swadlincote, lost in their own world of conversation, until Dora stopped. "Where's that sound comin' from Flo?" she said.

"It sounds like Town'all end," said Flo and they hurried towards the delph.

"Eh up Flo, look what's 'ere! It's one of them school bands. Let's stop and listen for a bit." Flo put her shopping bags down and they stood among the crowd, enjoying the musical entertainment of the Pingle School Big Band.

"Eh, that teks ya back a bit," said Dora. "There were always somat cracking off onth delph." "Arr, looks like it's still thsame. I'm glad I'n com back," said Flo.

They stood together, oblivious of the time, until the sky overhead darkened.

"It's startin' to reen," said Dora. "Way'd better be gooin. I enner got me brolly, en yo?" "No," said Flo, picking up her shopping and striding out for home.

Every now and then, a special kind of person comes along and their caring attitude touches the heart and becomes an inspiration to others. Age has no distinction. This special kind of person could be as young as five years old and a few years ago, one such person came to the notice of Ester Rantzen and that person was Joanna Parkinson - Hardman; from Church Gresley - Swadlincote.

Joanna became a fundraiser for Imperial Cancer when she was five. It was at the time when her mother was battling the disease. Joanna wanted to show even at that tender age that she cared and wanted to help and so she was able to raise eight hundred pounds by selling her toys and games, inspiring her friends, family and neighbours to help.

When she was ten years old, Joanna was inspired to write poems and sell them in aid of the Imperial Cancer Research. She became an inspiration to other distinguished writers and celebrities whose poems were entered in a book with Joanna's poems, entitled 'POEMS BY JOANNA PARKINSON - HARDMAN and some friends. It went into print in 1992 by BBC Books, in time for the BBC TV Hearts of Gold programme in which Joanna herself, was honoured. Joanna's poems played their part and accomplished much and whatever else she may not achieve in life, as she enters the world now as a young woman of seventeen; that time seven years ago, was special for Joanna.

They used to have Swadlincote Amateur Operatics Society and they used to put all Gilbert and Sullivan on. Mondays, they had a dress rehearsal and they allowed the school children to go and watch. I was about eleven or twelve and I saw 'PATIENCE' and 'QUAKER GIRL' but I never saw 'THE PIRATES OF PENZANCE'

That was a long time ago you say, but we haven't got anything like that today in Swadlincote. Hey! Let's not be too hasty. What we DO have is a Swadlincote singer, dancer and all-round performer. Andrew Booth - stage name Drew Charles. He is a young man in his 20's. Well known and well thought of. Andrew is in partnership with Reg Yates at the 'Visage' Hair Salon in Hearthcote Road, Swadlincote.

I first read about this young man in 1997, when he played the title role of 'Barnum' at Barry Youngs Stardust Theatre, near Coalville. The Tale of Barnum follows the larger than life career of Phineas T. Barnum, the flamboyant, self styled World's Greatest Showman.

In 1998 andrew won a prestigious International Character Award for a stunning performance in an updated version of Gilbert and Sullivan's, 'PATIENCE' at the Buxton International Festival; followed by a return to the Stardust Theatre, for a one off show.

Andrew's success includes several appearances on television and local radio and he released an album of original material in Spring 1999. When I asked Andrew what type of music he likes singing best, he said. "Mainly, modern Opera type music." That's not surprising really, since he was influenced by his mother who belonged to the Burton Opera Society. Andrew certainly is a 'Star in the Making.'

Swadlincote is a place that isn't on a main road. It's bypassed by main roads. It's in some ways a back water, but in this back water, lots of things have evolved through the mining, and pottery business.

Things that have been made here, have been exported all over the world in this back water that isn't on a main railway line, and wasn't on a main railway line. They had to put a loop through it. But when they did, the goods and the cost which were carried on it was fantastic. It was one of the richest railway lines in the country, because of what was carried on it, from the mining and pottery industries, but people who lived here were always proud to say, "Yes, I come from Swad."

HISTORY IN THE MAKING • 177

1992 Joanna Parkinson-Hardman

1999 Andrew Booth (Stage name Drew Charles)

178 • INTO THE LIGHT 2000

1999 Jennie Summerbell, Ballet Dancer

1999 Carl Jones

Another of our stars is making headway into the world of Ballet. Years ago, in the 40' and 5o's, there was little thought given to Ballet among school children in the Swadlincote area, mainly because the nearest School of Ballet was in Burton, a large room near the Electric Cinema in the High Street, run by a Mrs Lake. There were two of us from Woodville School, who, after seeing a few photographs of Ballet stars, went to see if we'd got what it takes.

Our first day there, was a bit of a shock, when Mrs Lake said. "Pull your skirts up dears, so I can look at your legs. We had been brought up real prim and proper and so we lifted our skirts to calf length. "Higher dears," said Mrs Lake, "above the knees." My friend looked at me and our knees began to knock. Anyway, we giggled a lot on the bus going home as we related to our parents what had happened.

We only went about three times, it took far too long to get there and back on the bus, our parents didn't have a car between them back then in the 40's.

Things are a lot better now and to watch Swanlake on stage is magic and 'The Red Shoes' on Cinema screen. No wonder our young star, 13year old Jennie Summerbell from Swadlincote, has taken to Ballet shoes and a Tutu.

Jennie has achieved an outstanding result in a recent Elementary Ballet exam she took at the Lucy Heafield School of Dance. Jennie has gained a 90% pass, which is excellent.

This high grade means that she can take part in a scholarship Class in Manchester, pitting her talents against 200 other ballerinas from around the country. This will take place in March - year 2000.

Jennie knows that it takes a lot of hard work and dedication to reach the top, but her long range hope is that eventually, she will be able to open her own Ballet School in Swadlincote.

Go for it Jennie, Swadlincote is behind you all the way!

One young man is well on the way to realising his ambitions.

Butlin's 'Redcoat,' Carl Jones, from Plummer Road, Newhall, Swadlincote, was picked as a presenter for the morning programme to be shown at the Company's holiday camp in Skegness.

The filming is part of a new Butlins initiative and Carl and his co-presenter were chosen for the job out of 150 other hopefuls at the holiday centre. Carl said."I'm really excited about it. Everybody wants the job, because everybody's got aspirations of being famous. We are going to be shown on television just at Butlins, but if we get any Scouts, the first people they see will be the presenters. All this is heady stuff and happened so fast. But where did it all start?

"He doesn't get it from me or his dad," said his mum, because his dad's a quiet man. It may have started from as far back as Junior School. They did a 'Jim'll fix it' and Carl was in that. Then at the Senior School, they did a Fashion show and Carl had it in mind to be a male model, but then they did 'Grease' at school and he was sure that one day, he would be on television.

As Carl grew up, he was trained as a joiner, then one day he said he was fed up with an every day job, so, off he went backpacking in Australia, with four others and he worked for a while at a fire-door factory. Later, Carl sold encyclopedias in the outback (there must be some very knowledgeable Kangaroos out there) because, at one point Carl said they went 36hours across Australia, without seeing a soul, but they slept under the stars and that was fantastic," said Carl.

Of course he made friends in Australia and they still keep in touch.

When he came back, he went to Derby for an interview for a Butlin 'Red' as they are called now (in the 50's they were known as Redcoats) and he got on, so now Carl is at Skegness.

He compared a new year show at Butlins and while he was on stage, he introduced the crowd to his parents who were in the audience and thanked them for what they had done for him. No wonder his parents are proud - Carl sounds quite a lad!

On the day that the South Derbyshire Writers Group launched the cassette 'SOUNDS LIKE SWAD' at the Town Hall, in Swadlincote, March 17th 1998 11am. Swadlincote had another event in the afternoon which was of great interest to all budding writers. Top television Script writer Lucy Gannon paid Swadlincote a visit.

About thirty people including three of us from the South Derbyshire Writers Group, looked forward to meeting Lucy at the Swadlincote Library and after she had told us all something of her own life and the very popular programmes she had created - Peak Practice, Bramwell and Soldier, Soldier, we were able to ask her many questions about writing. She even gave us a sneak preview of her next project, which was Hope and Glory, with Lenny Henry playing a straight role.

We all very much appreciated the afternoon spent with Lucy and as she returned to her home in Wirksworth, she took a little bit of old Swad back with her to play in the car - the cassette we had launched that morning, 'SOUNDS LIKE SWAD.'

1998 Polly Jemison with Lucy Gannon, Swadlincote Library

The Millennium Dawns

There I sat in my office, working away at my computer. I typed in the file name of what I'd done, but my computer came back at me. 'Cannot create, 'so, from that I knew my disc was full. I hurriedly reached for a new disc and proceeded to ask the computer to delete the file that couldn't be completed, but when I checked later, I found it hadn't deleted the file.

I was annoyed and requested it again to delete the file, in other words - Do it or else! You're only a flippin' computer. However, next day, the computer got back at me, it wouldn't even let me get into it at all. I tried everything I could think of, but it was no use. Then I panicked - What to do!

I looked through the phone book, dialled and shouted, HELP!

"Bring everything you've got with you. I'll take a look at it," said the man who obviously knew more about computers than I did.

I sat there, chewing my nails, watching him press all the buttons without success. "It sure is having a real sulk," he said, as if the computer had a mind of its own. He pressed a few more buttons, then bingo! it began to work.

"What was the problem," I asked, when he'd got it running smoothly. "A corrupted file," he said. But as I drove home with the computer in the back of the car, I had this overwhelming feeling that it was really alive and had developed a mind of its own. 'Just let it try.' I thought, 'I'll show it who's Boss!'

On August 11th.1999, at 11 minutes, 11 seconds past 11am, it was to be the UK's first total solar eclipse for 72 years. The best place to experience totality was Cornwall.

Already, on the Friday before, the television news was encouraging those who were going to see it, to go before Wednesday, because the traffic would be nose to tail.

Also, people were being warned not to look at the sun without eye protection, even a few seconds without, could harm the eyes.

The eclipse of the sun is said to be the 'Grandest' sight in all nature. The sun's diameter is 400 times that of the moon and the sun is also 400 times further away than the moon; that is why the two appear almost exactly the same size when the earth, moon and sun line up, with the moon in the middle position. The dark mass of the moon blots out the bright disc of the sun and we have an eclipse.

At 10.50am the light begins to fade. Flowers may close up and animals will settle as if for an early night. Dogs may howl. Then just minutes before totality, the land will be bathed in a greyish light and the temperature may fall dramatically.

Pets should be kept indoors away from the windows, because their eyes might be damaged. The twilight before the eclipse will offer a rare chance to see the planet Mercury. It will be about as far to the west as the brilliant shining Venus is to the east. But did it really happen that way.

Well, in Cornwall, where they were able to experience totality, it was cloudy, which hindered the viewing of the eclipse. However, like everywhere else, they had television as a back up and no one missed anything. The crowds on the beaches, gasped, as the light began to fade, leaving an eerie glow. Then they felt the sudden darkness that descended upon them and the cold, as the temperature dropped.

The shouts of excitement as the moons shadow began to hide the sun, changed to a hush as it disappeared altogether and they all waited with bated breath for the sun to re-appear. When it did, there was flash of light and the diamond ring effect was stunning and as the sun in all its glory re-appeared in full, the cheers went up and the partying began.

Some of those who had witnessed the eclipse in 1927, had travelled down to Cornwall this time to see it and although they were well on in years, they were just as overwhelmed by it all, as they had been when they were young.

Those of us who were not able to go down to Cornwall and not living in the area of totality, relied on television to see the Grandest sight in all nature and wished that we could be around to see the next one. Perhaps some of you felt the same way.

DERBYSHIRE DIALECT

In Swad the other day, I overheard one woman say to another.
"Ar thee geein owt awee?"
"If thee ar," she replied.
"theer kapin it for thesens."

Winter-time can be pretty bleak,
but not so in Swadlincote.
If you need cheering up,
take a walk down the
brightly lit centre,
and you will experience
a rare mixture of old and
modern, living side by side;
with buskers in the streets,
and roast potatoes and hot
chestnuts available for all.
The Fair also is often there,
in winter-time and the
laughing faces of children
reminds us of ourselves and
we smile at our thoughts
as we pass them by.

When I settled to the task of putting together, my thoughts about South Derbyshire, I reflected on the first and then the lasting impressions over the last nine years that I have been involved in local politics. Unusually, the two views came up with the same themes.

First and most important, friendliness. As a newcomer I noticed straight away how easy it was to talk; how willing people were to help, how a smile and a greeting was natural. How straightforward views were and how even disagreement was friendly. South Derbyshire still retains a strong community identity, but, unusually, it is a community spirit that welcomes most outsiders. The long period of mining migration with miners and their families arriving from distant parts of Britain, must have had something to do with that, but the same spirit persists now. I regularly contrast the sheer reasonableness of people here with stories I hear from other MPs of tense and traumatic encounters with constituents.

Second, time and scale. Compared to the pace of life in a big city, time moves a touch slower here, people have longer to talk. I feel that strongly as I re-enter

South Derbyshire after a few days in London. The gentle landscapes, the time it takes to travel from place to place in the area, the small scale of communities and of most businesses. The fact that many businesses are locally owned, all lend a sense that some of the rapid pace of change of the last few decades has been accepted more selectively here and that people still have time for each other.

Third, beauty. Although parts of South Derbyshire retain the scars of it's heritage as a centre of coal, clay and gravel extraction, the mix of lowland livestock farming, river valley contours, small villages, country houses and their parklands and industrial heritage; produce many areas of outstanding beauty. Again the scale is important - we don't have the dramatic scenery of the Peaks, but a more gentle landscape on a human scale. Many visiting politicians comment on this as I escort them round the area.

Finally, heritage. South Derbyshire is proud of its history and there are plenty of long memories about. This book itself - continuing one of the most successful local history projects I have ever heard of - shows that. There are plenty of examples of our industrial heritage; although, more needs to be done to set them in a context where everyone can enjoy them. We also retain several attractive country houses and parks, often built and occupied by the owners of those industries.

It is a genuine pleasure and a privilege for me to represent South Derbyshire and its people. It is with relief that I return from the fevered atmosphere of London and start to experience the human values you find here.

The people in the Swadlincote area who lived through the Mining times, the Clay works, and the Pipe works, have brought about a special kind of person. They will speak their mind, but they'll do anything for you, and living in a time under such dangerous conditions, it bred into them a way of coping with that danger and whatever life threw at them. They never lost their sense of humour, and their zest for life. They are basically a happy people and remain so to this day.

Children love to be part of things and at the National Forest Festival in June 1999; people were encouraged to collect seeds and plant trees to celebrate the new millennium.

The National Forest project is now well under way and the young saplings that have been planted in our local area, will grow into hardy trees, offering the district of Swadlincote a lasting legacy for generations to come.

When people hear that I work at a National Forest Visitors Centre, the first thing they often say is 'We've seen all these signs for the National Forest but where are all the trees?' I try to look as though I'm not repeating myself - but in fact I've spent the past five years answering that question. It is getting easier to convince people.

Around 1.2 million baby trees have been planted in the district of South Derbyshire since the National Forest scheme was first set up by the Country Side Commission in 1991 - so now there are more trees than people.

At Rosliston Forestry Centre, where I am based, they are just starting to emerge from beneath the shelter of the hedgerows. You can begin to see what the future will look like; instead of tripping over the saplings, you can play 'hide and seek' among them.

It seems appropriate that, like the wealth of the district in the past and present - through extraction industries and farming - the future is rooted firmly in the soil. However, I can't imagine that the South Derbyshire of the future will be as part of some kind of forest theme park for visitors. Anyone at the National Forest Company would tell you that their vision is much broader than that - wishing to create a forest for us to enjoy living and working in as well as for the visitors.

Nothing anywhere ever stays the same for ever. So really the tree planting and the other habitat creation is about taking control of the changes and how the landscape develops.

It also makes a statement about our commitment to the natural environment - in such trouble in so many places in the world. That's what I tell myself every time I go out tree planting in the pouring rain! Think Global Act Local!

It is always exciting to witness changes. Even in the short time I have lived in Swadlincote there have been many, from new roundabouts appearing almost over night to new industry locating to the area. Everytime I've been away for a while I notice something new when I come home. I hope next time I return from my journeying to find trains once again stopping at Castle Gresley...

Driving into town I've been mesmerised by the industrial buildings growing like shimmering living being. On a trip around Nadins opencast site I was astounded by the depth of coalface and surrounding cliff! I've also noticed the sudden disappearance of part of Drakelow Power Station - one of my favourite landmarks. Watch out for the development of a new landmark in the shape of Woodlands Forest Park...

There's a lot to be said for Swadlincote and district and the most remarkable aspect, is the way that the people have adapted to all the changes that over the years have taken place.

The most dramatic change was the demise of the coal and clay industry, which in the past had gouged and devalued the area; whilst Swadlincote itself, was heavily polluted from the acrid fumes belching from the local pottery kilns and coal burning fires.

Pollution was not such a 'dirty word' as it is nowadays. Where there was muck, there was work and it brought trade to the local shops; which in turn sold goods acceptable both in price as well as quality; satisfying the needs of the local community.

New shops have opened in the High Street, but without the prestige and aplomb of Salts. In fact there are few family businesses operating in the town. The name of the day is now Charity. Not just in Swadlincote, but all over Britain, from Rich Richmond to humble Humberside. They give a good service whichever way you look at it and the proceeds go to help many deserving charities.

The largest profit maker must be Sainsburys, situated on the edge of town and in the town itself we have Somerfield as well as Woolworths. We've lost out to Curry's. They moved on to a larger town. Like everywhere else we now have a range of shops selling an assortment of goods to clean, pamper, relax or perhaps invigorate our tired bodies. Gone are the tinbaths in front of the fire, carbolic soap and the homecoming of worn people with calloused hands.

The area has become part of the National Forest and in the ground once ravished by clay extraction, young trees are growing and our footsteps take us along trails where years ago men walked to work and slaved beneath the ground.

Swadlincote town centre is now a pedestrianised zone, with seats for people to rest and gossip to one another. The aroma of fish and chips still wafts tantalisingly down the High Street, mingling on its way with those from Indian and Chinese take aways.

The French pedestrianised a lot of their shopping centres some years ago and Ooh la la! they have now taken over the running of 'Swad Market.' Their first criteria has been to set up stalls back on the Delph, but neither Lenny Blankley, the Miss Harrisons, nor Bill Toon with his carpet stall, will be there, for they are sadly no longer with us.

The building of houses all round the perimeter of Swadlincote has brought in its wake, many new people and like so many places, the siting of a big name Supermarket, in this case Sainsbury's, has encouraged the growth of edge of town shopping habits.

As we move into the next century, will the spirit of Entente Cordiale mingle freely with our memories of the past, under the shadow of the Town Hall clock, with Time the Avenger written above it.

Only time will tell!

As this will be the last writing I shall do in this book, my hope is that it should be something worthy of all the preceding chapters. I would liken these previous sections to small parcels of words, to be opened and enjoyed, especially as the time of year is leading up to Christmas 1999 and the period we have all be waiting for, the millennium!

I think probably, we shall all be disappointed, because life does not change in a flash. The mills of God grind slowly and so do changes in world attitudes and leaders.

The year 2000, for myself, will be the same as all the others. Ring out the bells and a happy New Year to everyone, for the sake of Auld Lang Syne.

I hope all our readers enjoy the book as much as we have enjoyed compiling it. 'INTO THE LIGHT 2000' is a follow-up to our first book, 'OUT OF THE DARK,' and these titles, I hope, epitomise the progression of mankind going forward towards better times and a more promising future.

I had a letter from some old friends. Vernons, who emigrated to Australia more than 40 years ago. They wanted to thank me for sending the book on Swadlincote - 'OUT OF THE DARK'.

A niece out there who married Harry Redfern of Newhall, who is featured in the book, was delighted to read it. A nephew out there who married a Clamp from Gresley, was so interested, he wrote to Swadlincote Council for a second book and sent the money for the new one, 'INTO THE LIGHT 2000.' Shall we say, they haven't forgotten Swad.

Swadlincote is not a place, it's people. I have known some very friendly and kind people since I settled in the area in 1939. I feel sad when I read of vandalism in our villages. I would like to say to the perpetrators, think again, don't do it. There's plenty of room for teen-agers as well as we old ones. We were teen-agers once. The old saying 'Life is what you make it' should be 'Life is what you and others can make it.' Let's try and make it happy and worth remembering, for old and young, alike.

A COAT OF ARMS TO BE PROUD OF

I feel that this important heraldic devise is a proud possession that few people are aware of.

When in 1974, South Derbyshire District Council came into being, it embraced Swadlincote Urban District Council, Repton Rural District Council and part of South East Derbyshire Rural Council. A new Coat of Arms was approved by the Council, the College of Arms and formally accepted by our Council in 1976.

As with the old design approved in January 1947, Mr Ellis Tomlinson submitted his second shield after consultation with local historian, H T Wain.

So what does the shield represent? Heraldic terms are difficult to understand, so here is the plain man's version.

Heraldic terms are not easy to understand, so here is the plain man's version.

1. *The green background in the bottom half of the shield refers to agriculture. The sheaves were taken from the Arms of the Earl of Chester and associated with Calke and Repton in the 12^b century.*
2. *Three black rings in the lower half refer to the iron pipe industry and the union of the three Councils.*
3. *The gold chevron, outlined in black represent bricks and refers to the clay industry.*
4. *Flames issue out of a mould at the top of he shield a reference to the coal industry and the fire clay industry of Swadlincote.*
5. *The tower on the mound is taken from the Arms of the Stanhopes but shaped to represent the cooling towers of Drakelow and Willington.*

6. The supporters relate to the Gresley's: on the left, a lion. On the right a wolf, supporter of the Stanhopes. The Tudor on the shoulder of each beast is from the county Coat of Arms.

7. The motto in English 'The earth our wealth'

Our thanks to Philip Heath, Heritage Officer, South Derbyshire District Council.

Imagine, it is the morning of the very first day of January. The year - 2000. The town of Swadlincote awakes to a new day that is like no other. Everyone is in expectation of something never before experienced - the beginning of a new era.

Already, the town has been preparing to greet the millennium, by casting aside its old image and now it is ready.

Gone are the tall chimnies of the coal mines, the clayworks and most of the pottery works.

Gone are the slag heaps, the smoke and the sulphur fumes. The dirty windows and the black spotted washing hanging on the line. Look where you may, there is hardly a chimney in sight. The overall greyness of the town has gone and there is a much brighter outlook. Now we can see the green fields in the background, with places to walk, sit and enjoy the views.

From the old clay workings, we see young saplings growing, creating and extending the new National Forest, gradually, spreading through the green belt and bringing with it, a new way of life. This is surely a good start for the millennium.

The clock on the delph strikes nine in the morning and Tom, walks down to the shop for a newspaper. His mate Len, is already sitting on his favourite bench on the delph. "Ay up sorry," said Tom. "How ya doin? You're out early this mornin.'"

"I know," said Len. "I'n com out of our Ethel's road. Er's already watching telly and er reckons as I'n got to put a tie on this afternoon."

"What for?" said Tom.

"It's cos me sister's comin for tea and er enner got a telly, an' er wants to say what cracks off, an' ers a stickler for dressin' up.

"Well," said Tom, laughing.

"It might be a new millennium, but some things never change, do they!"

HISTORY IN THE MAKING • 191

1999 Swadlincote's Newsboard on the Delph, designed by local children

1999 The Delph Swadlincote